Anti Stress Adult Coloring Book

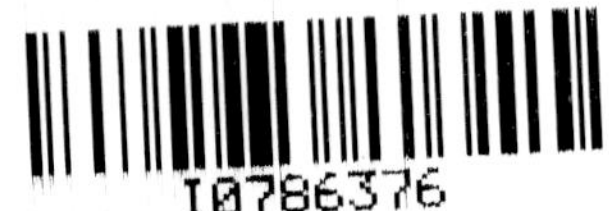

Copyright: Published in the United States by Peter Raymond
Published August 2018
ISBN-13: 978-1724854452
ISBN-10: 1724854453

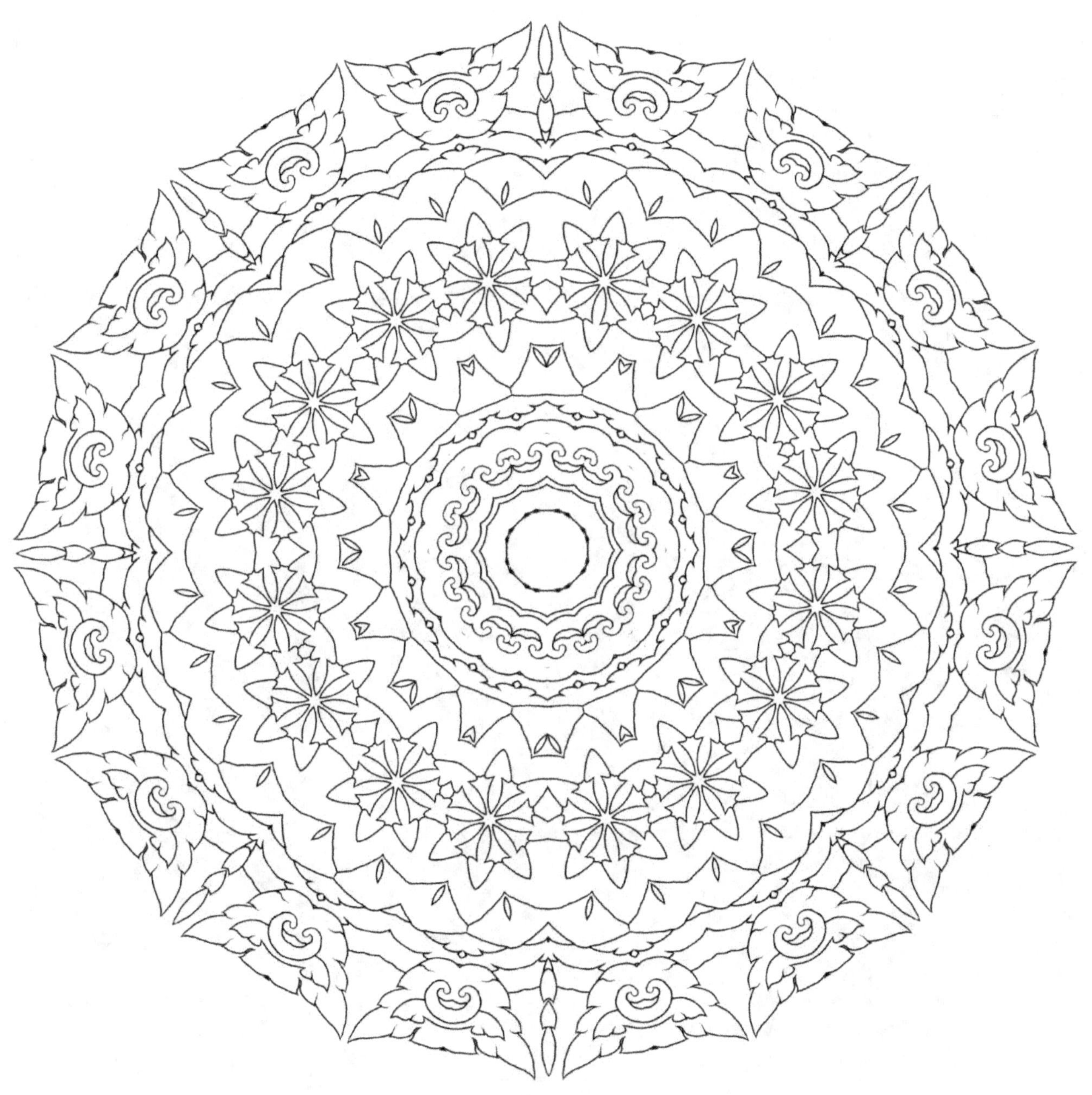

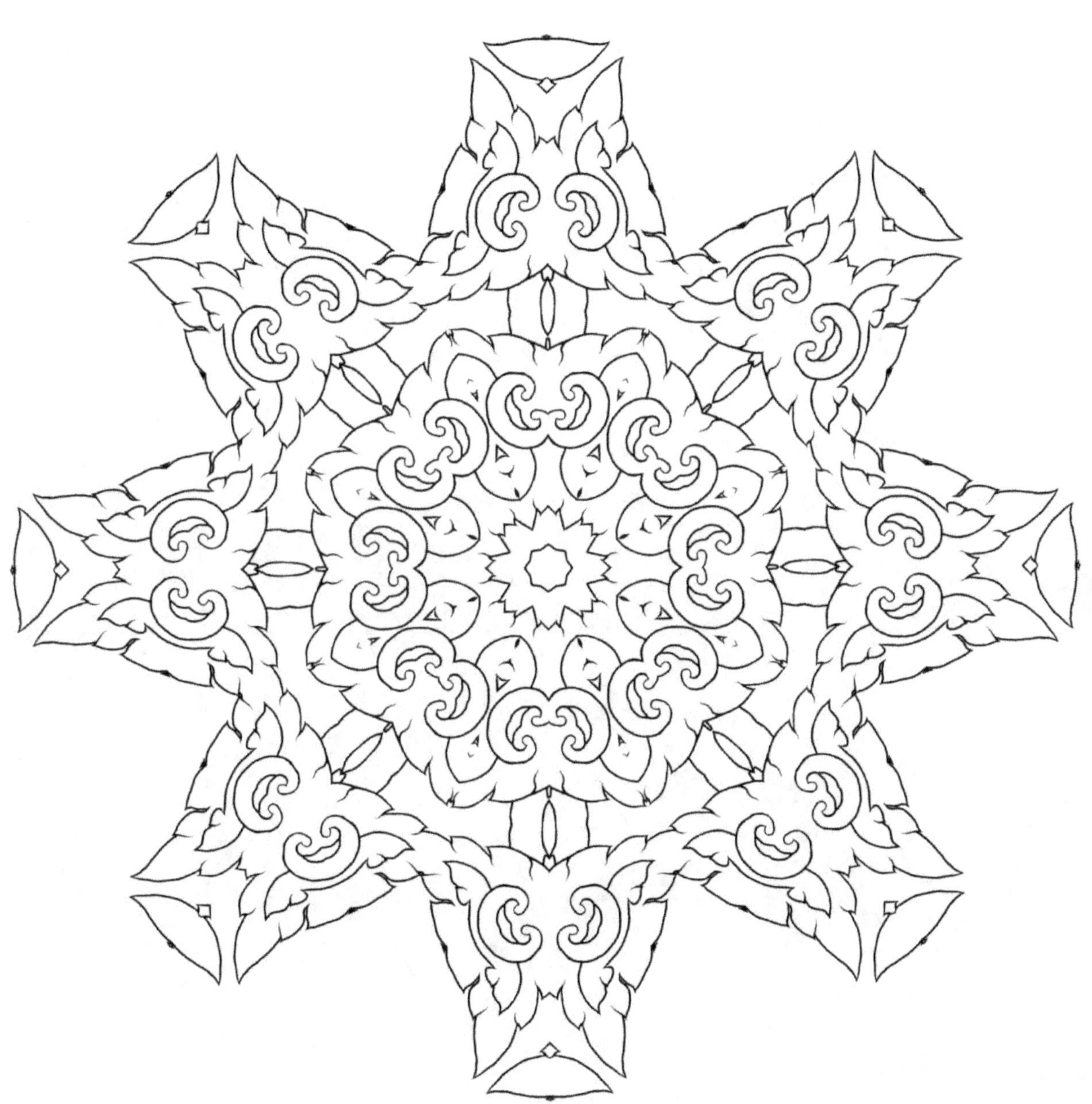

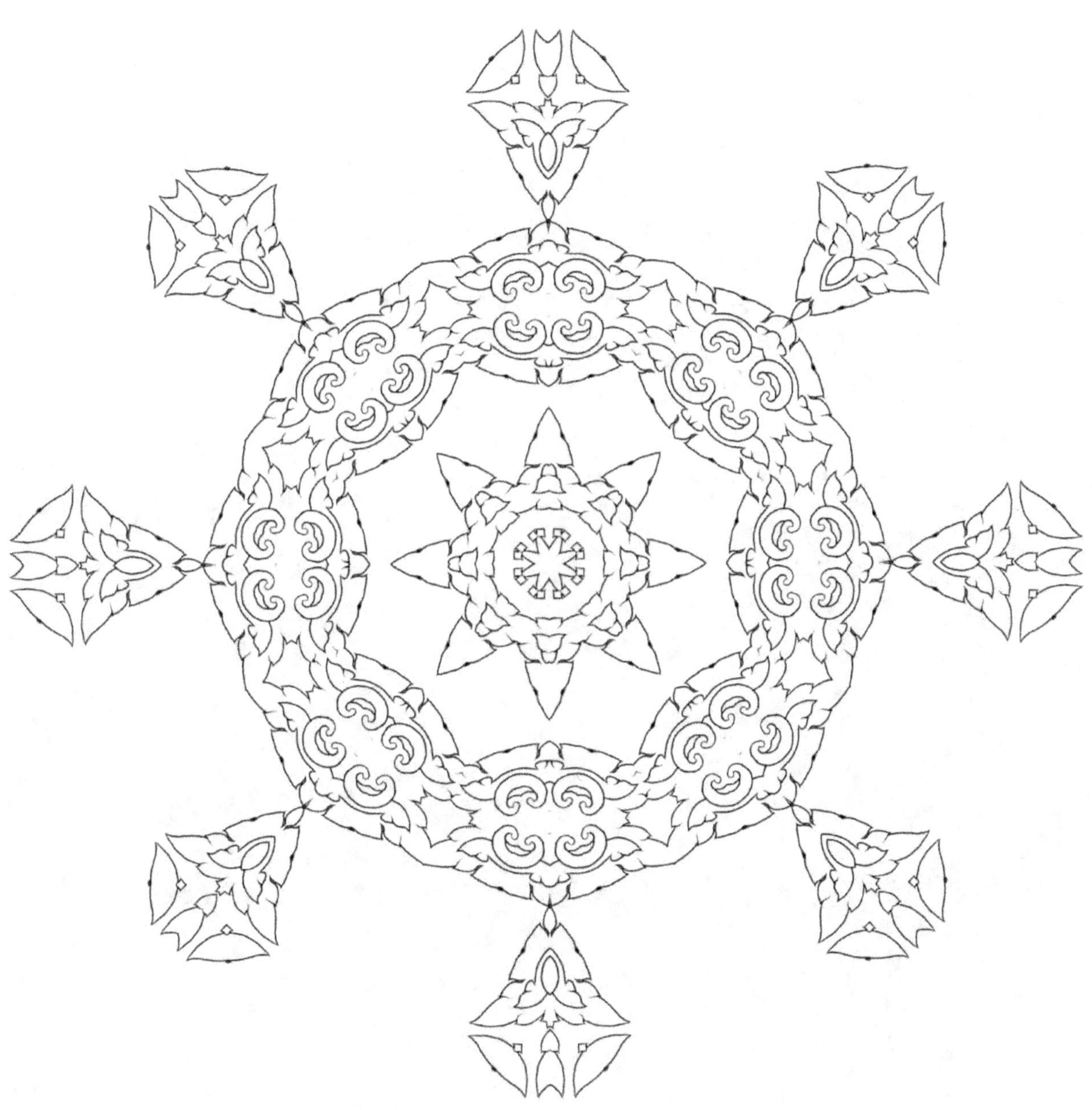

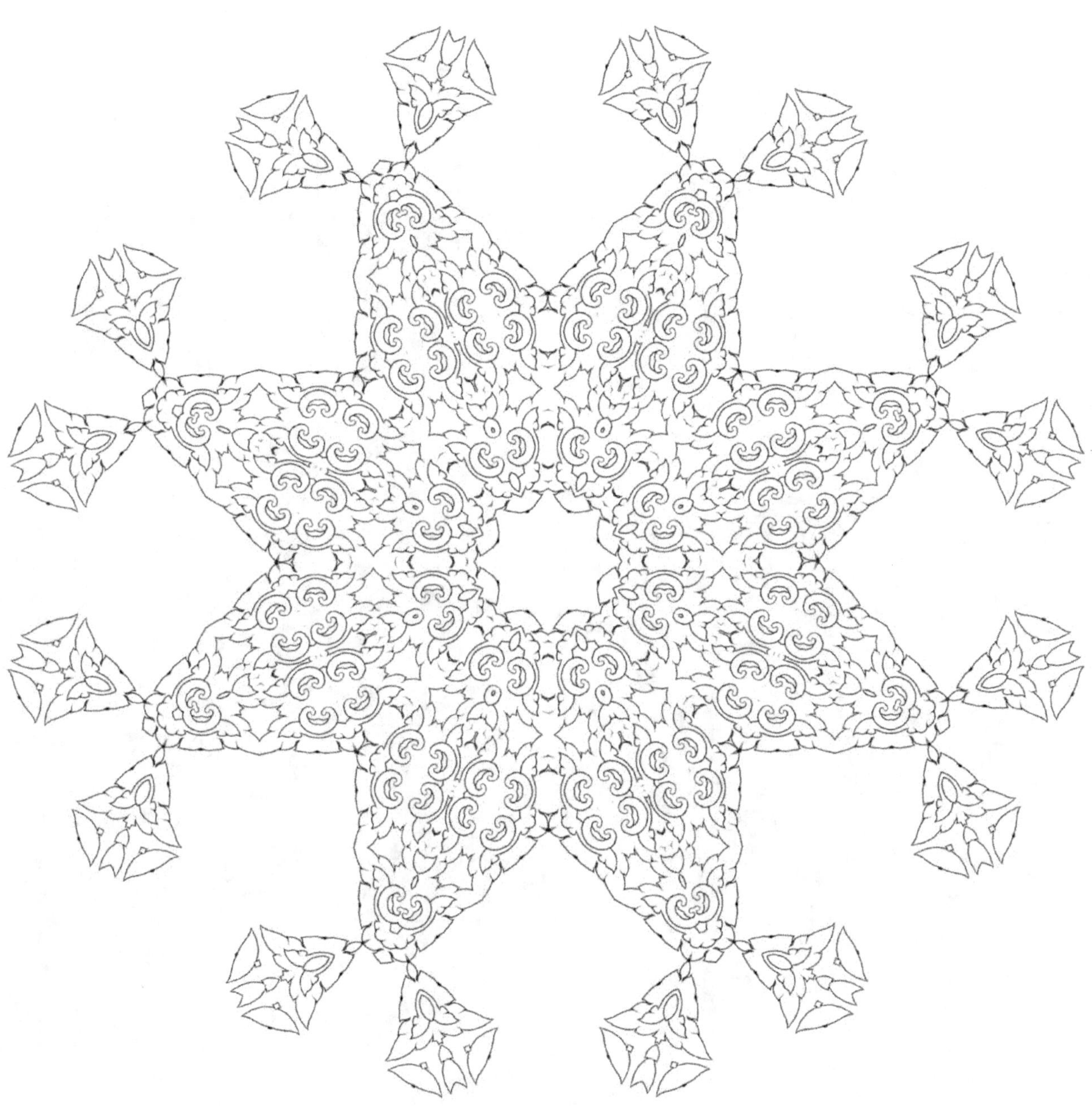

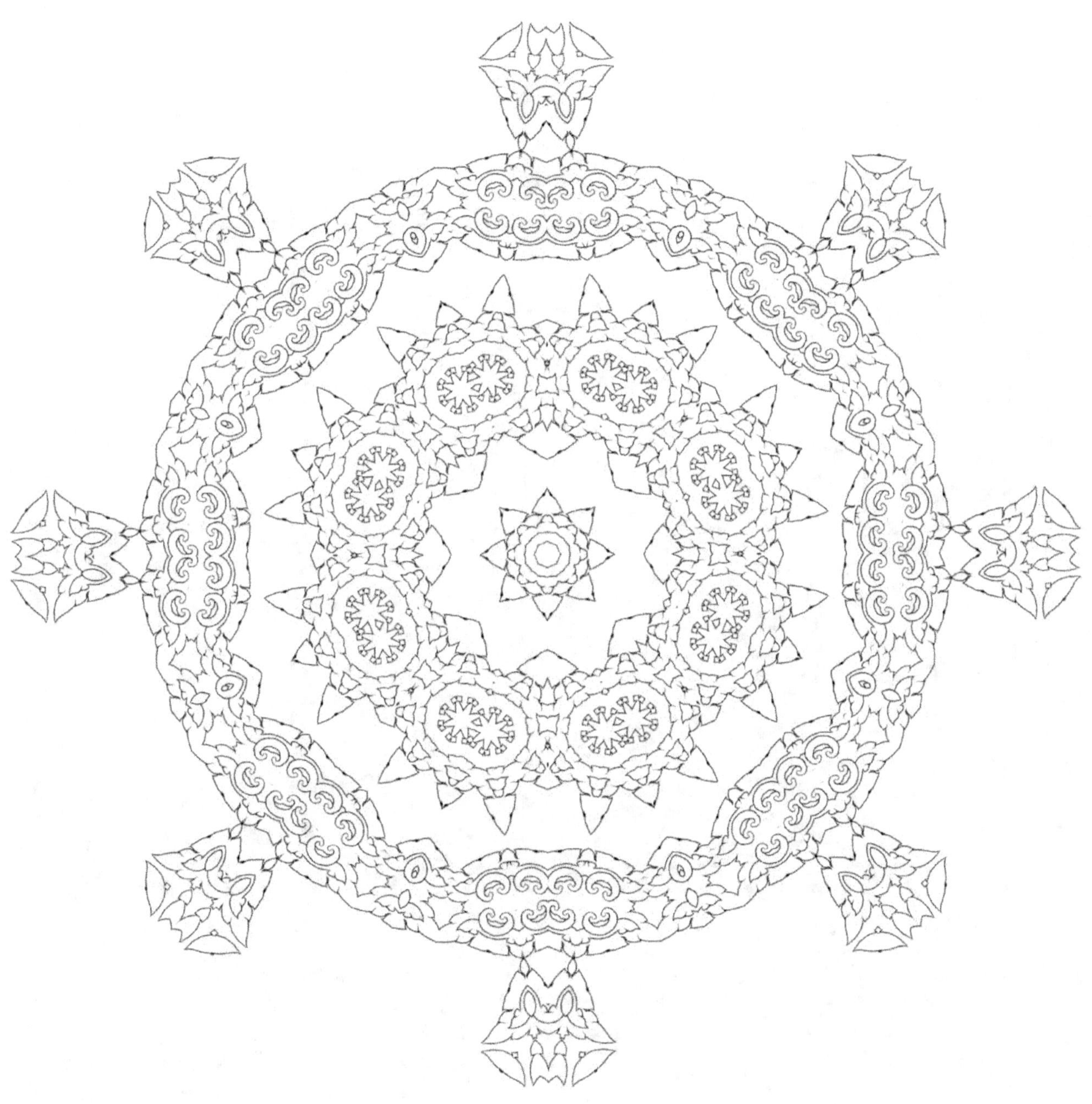

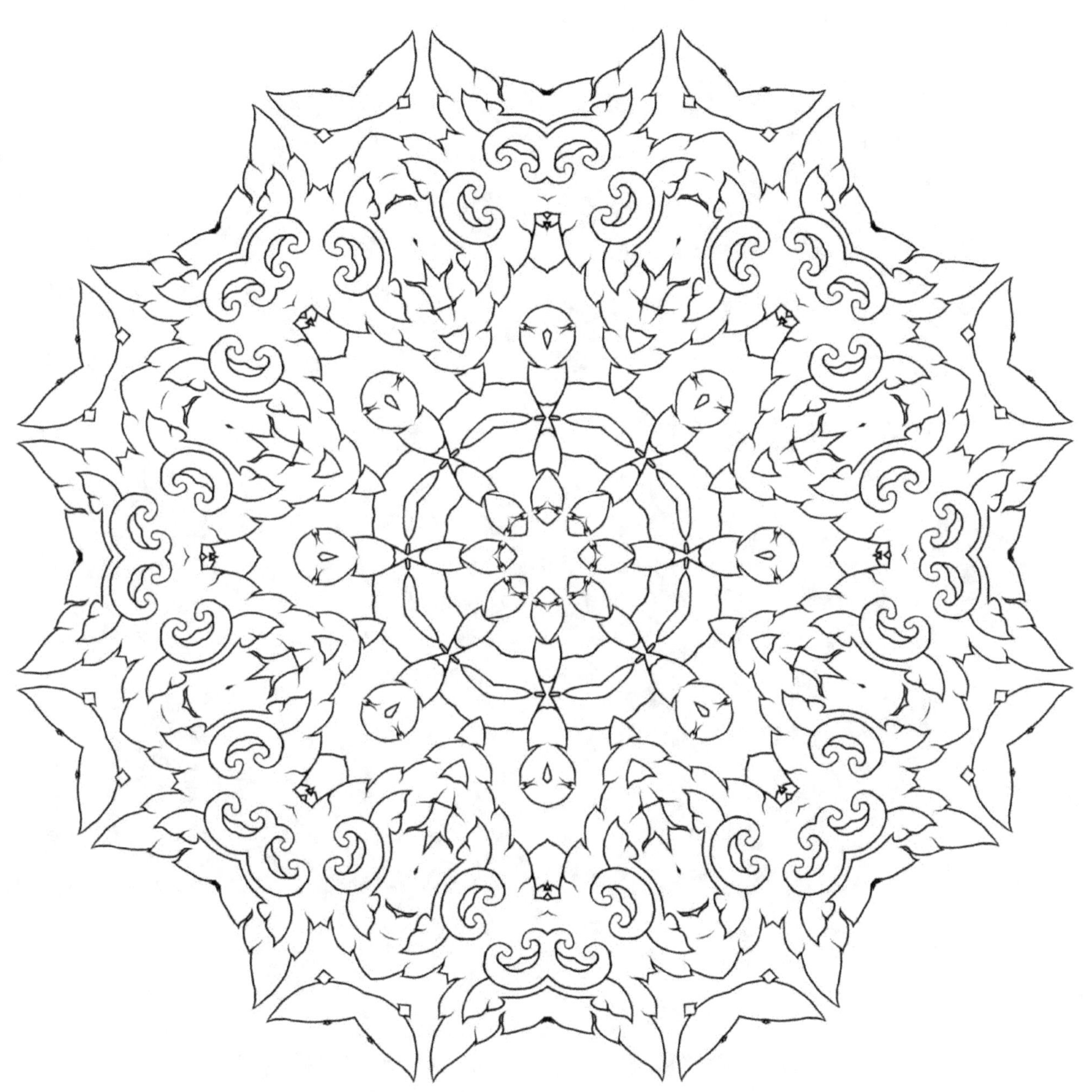

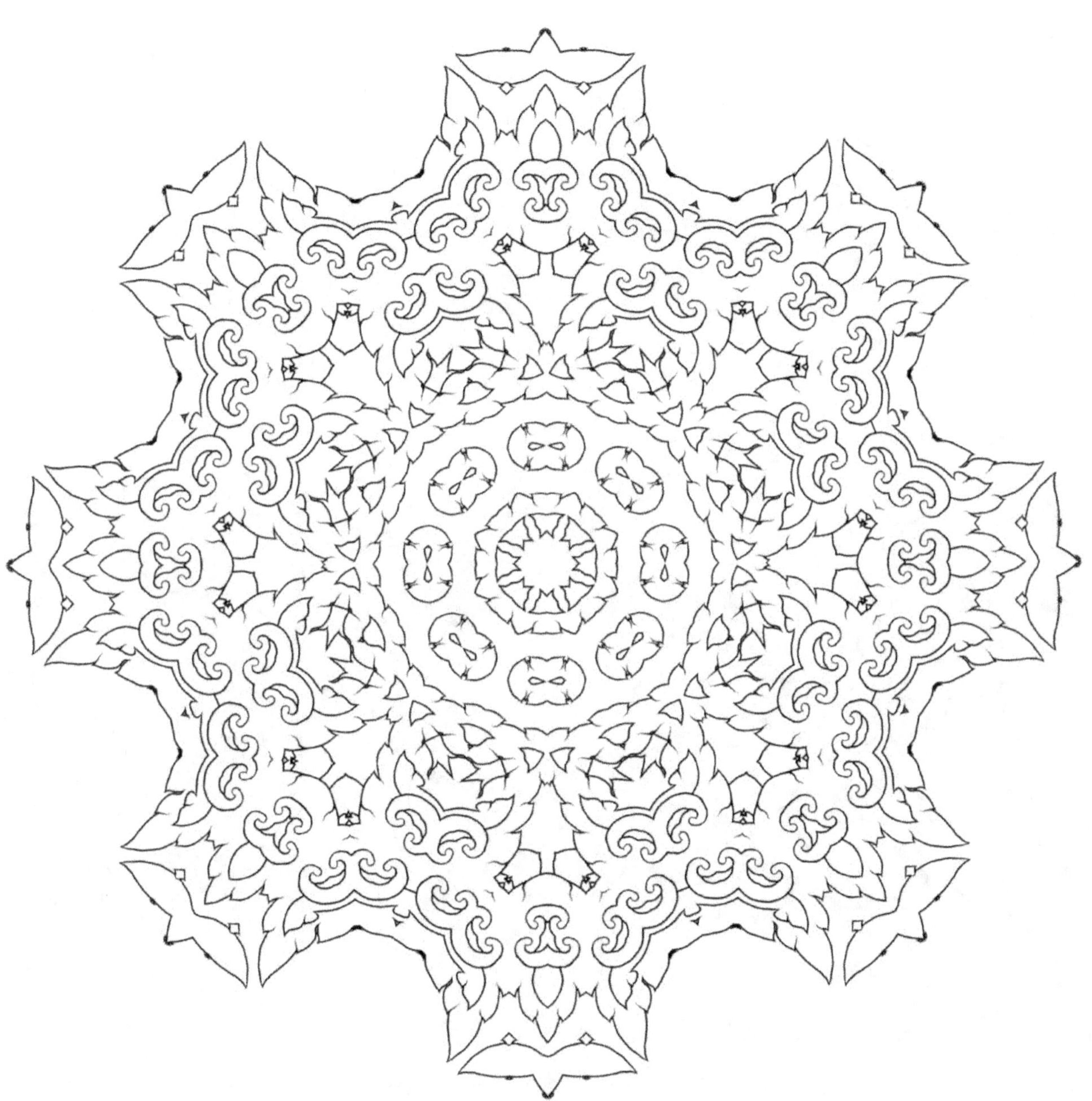

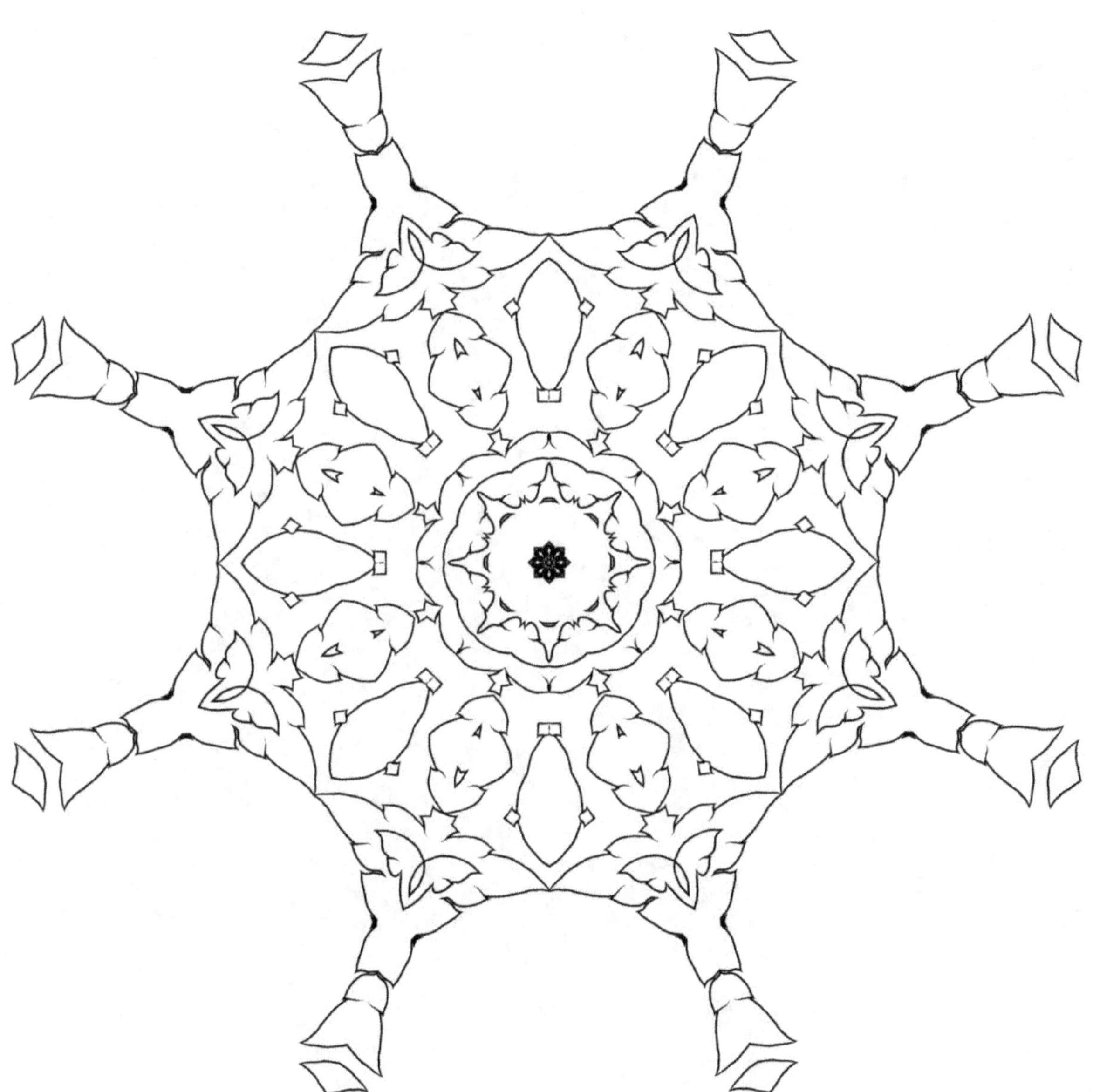

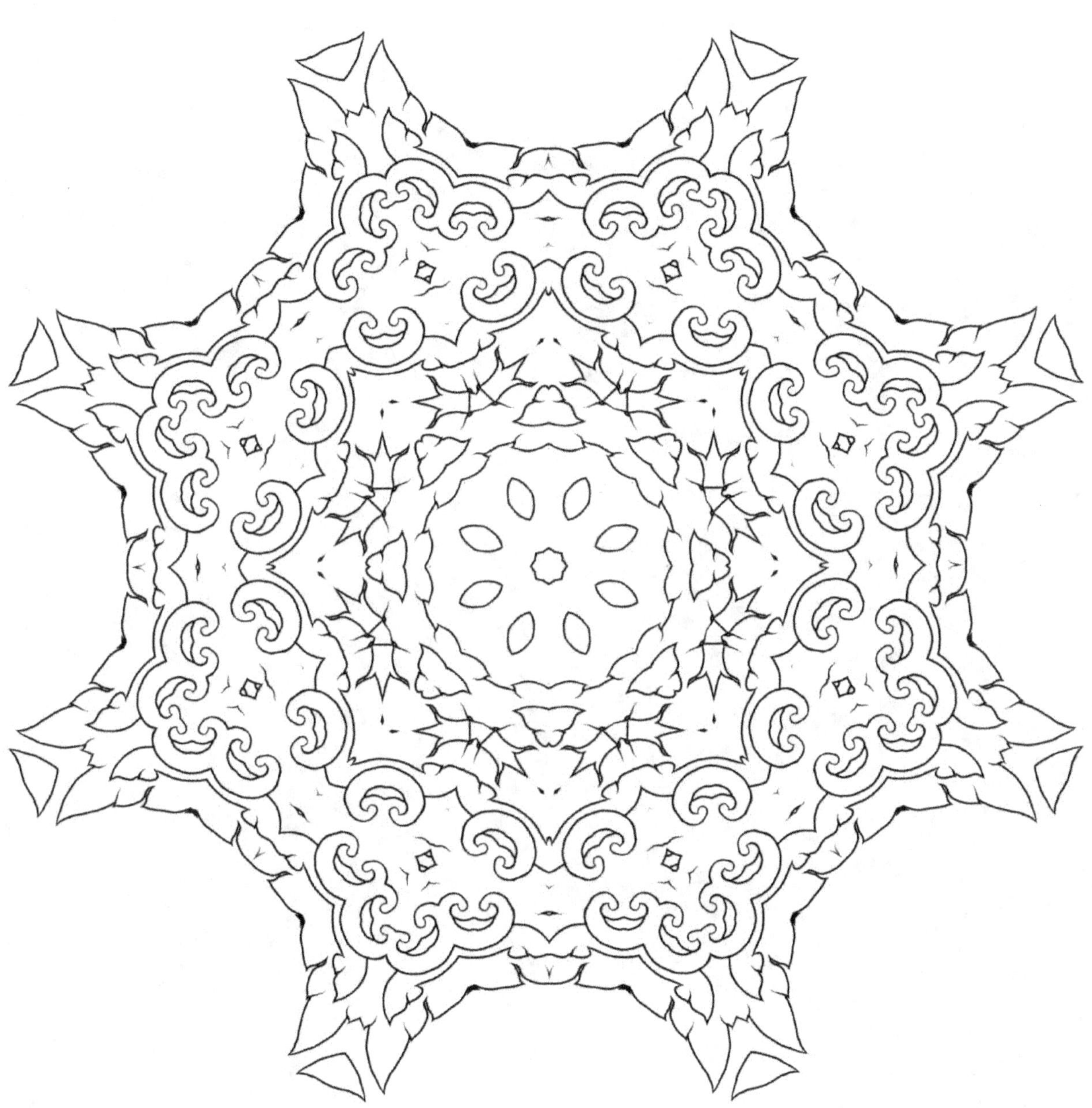

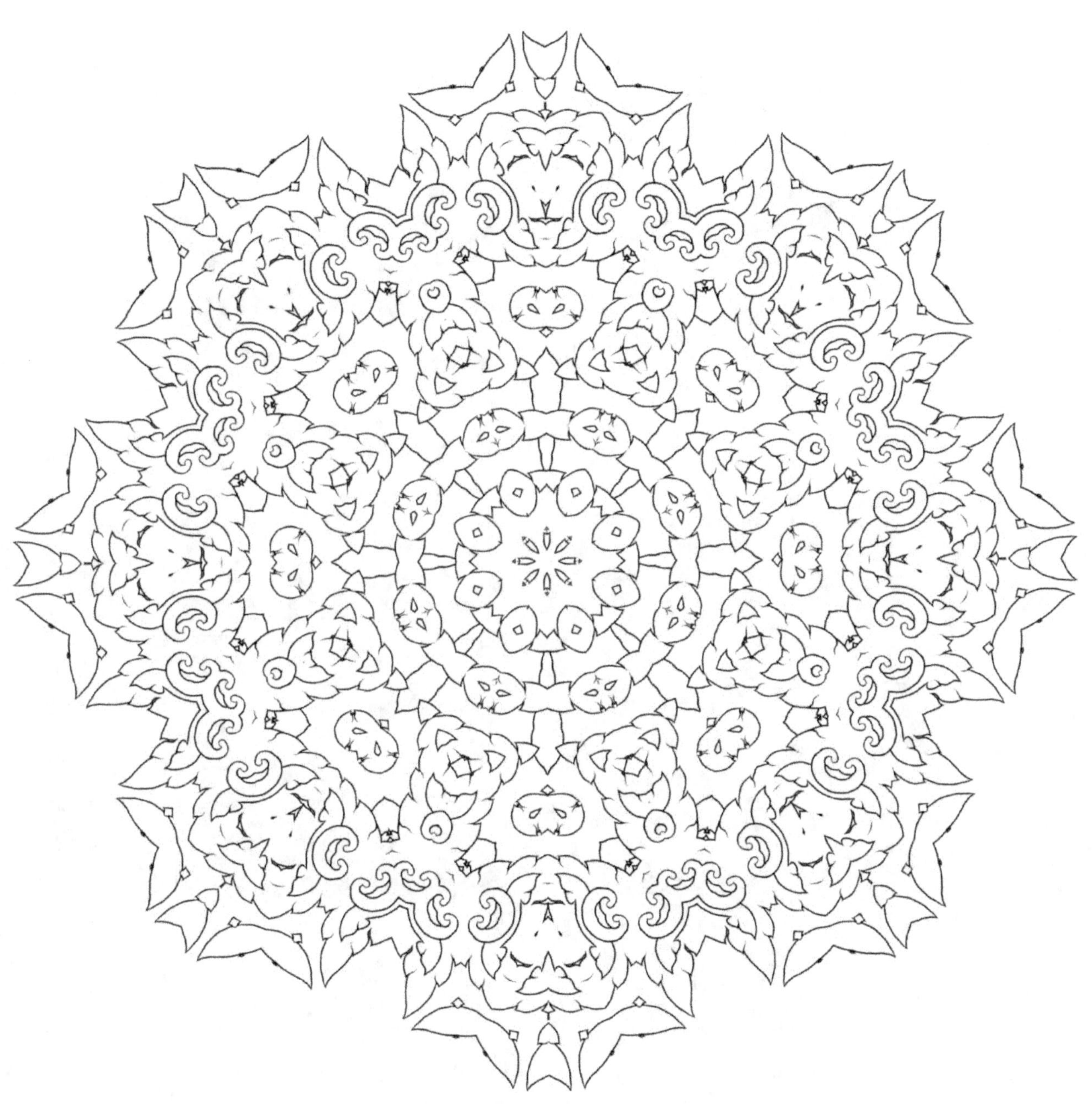

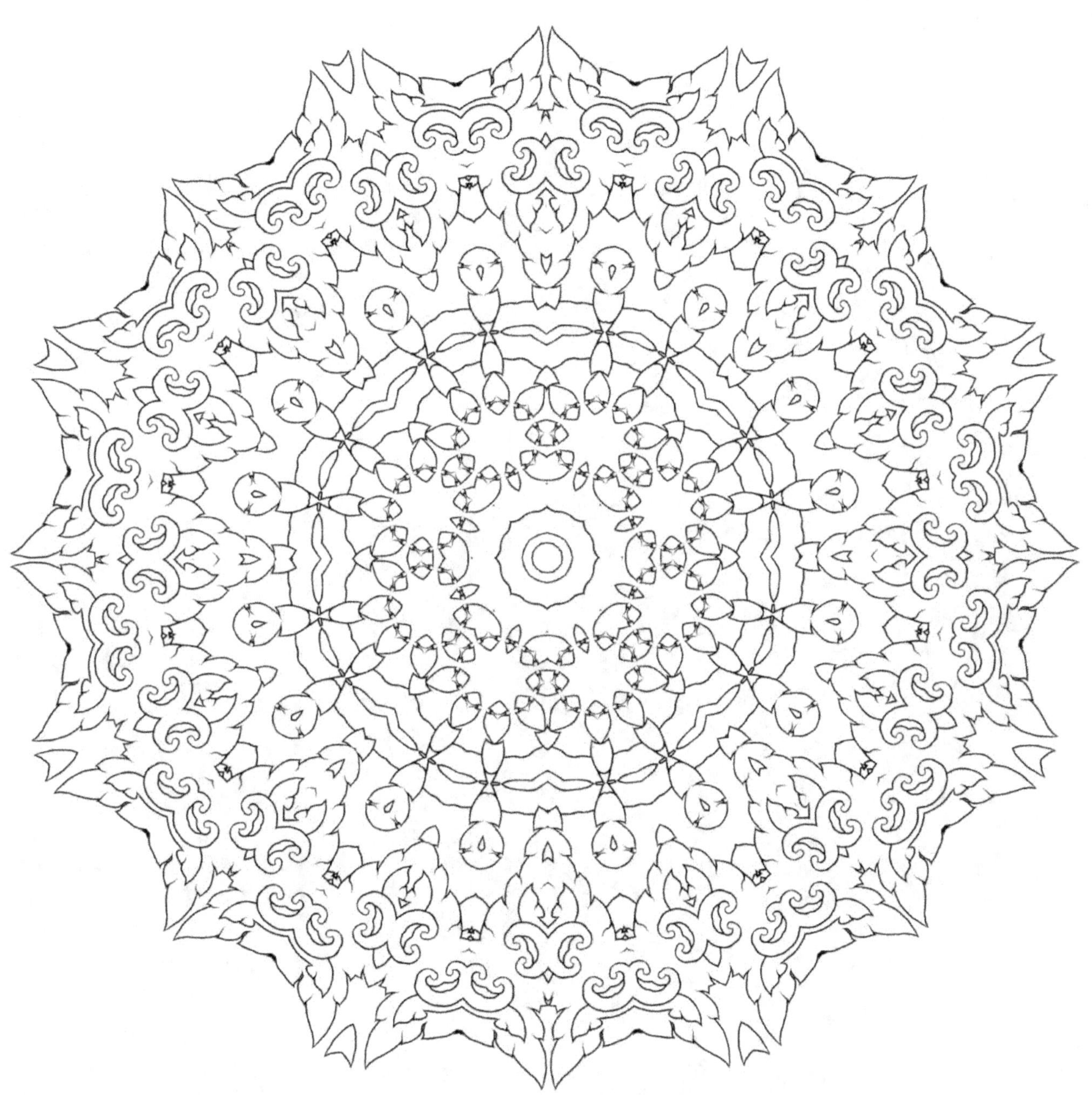

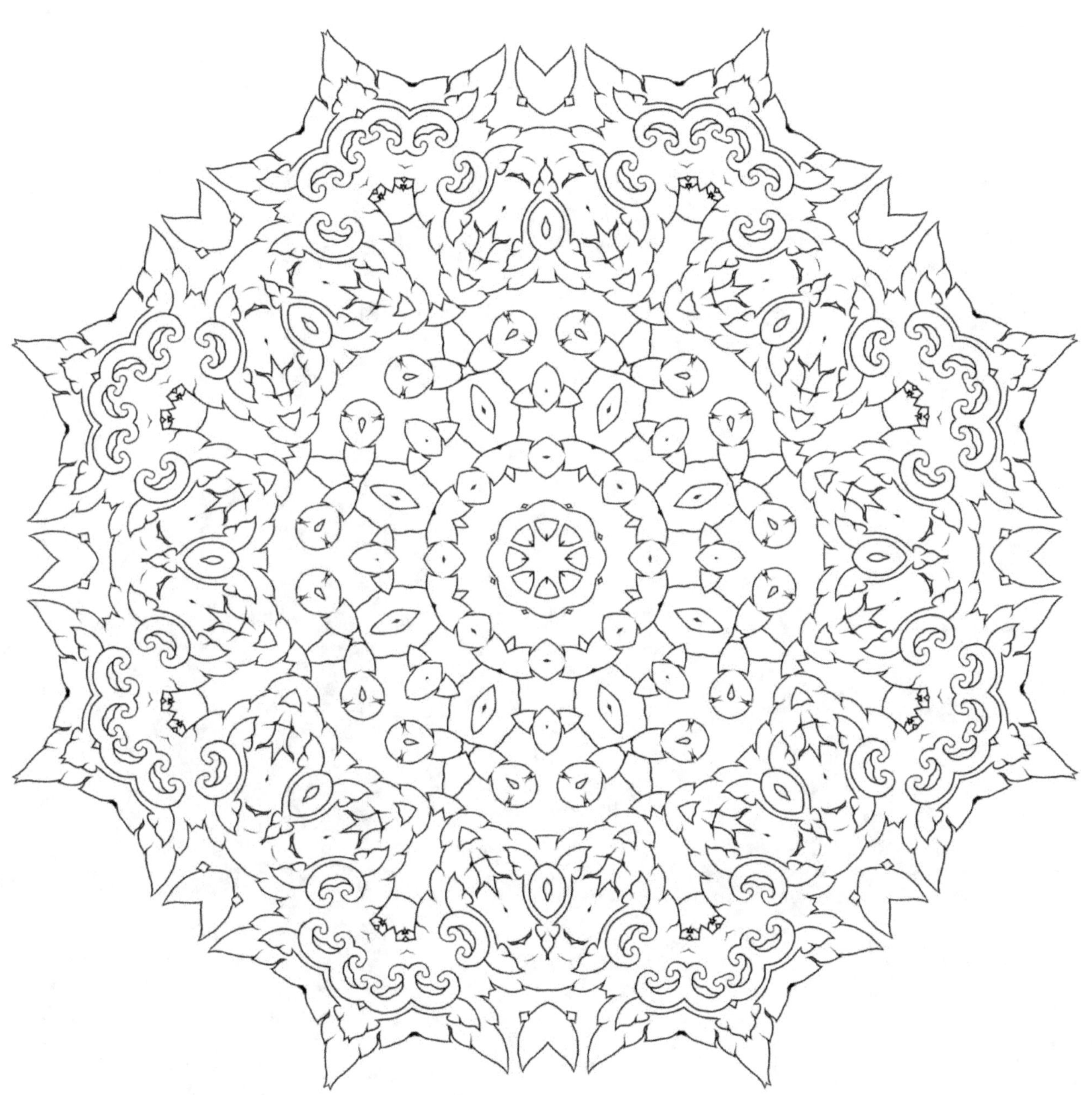

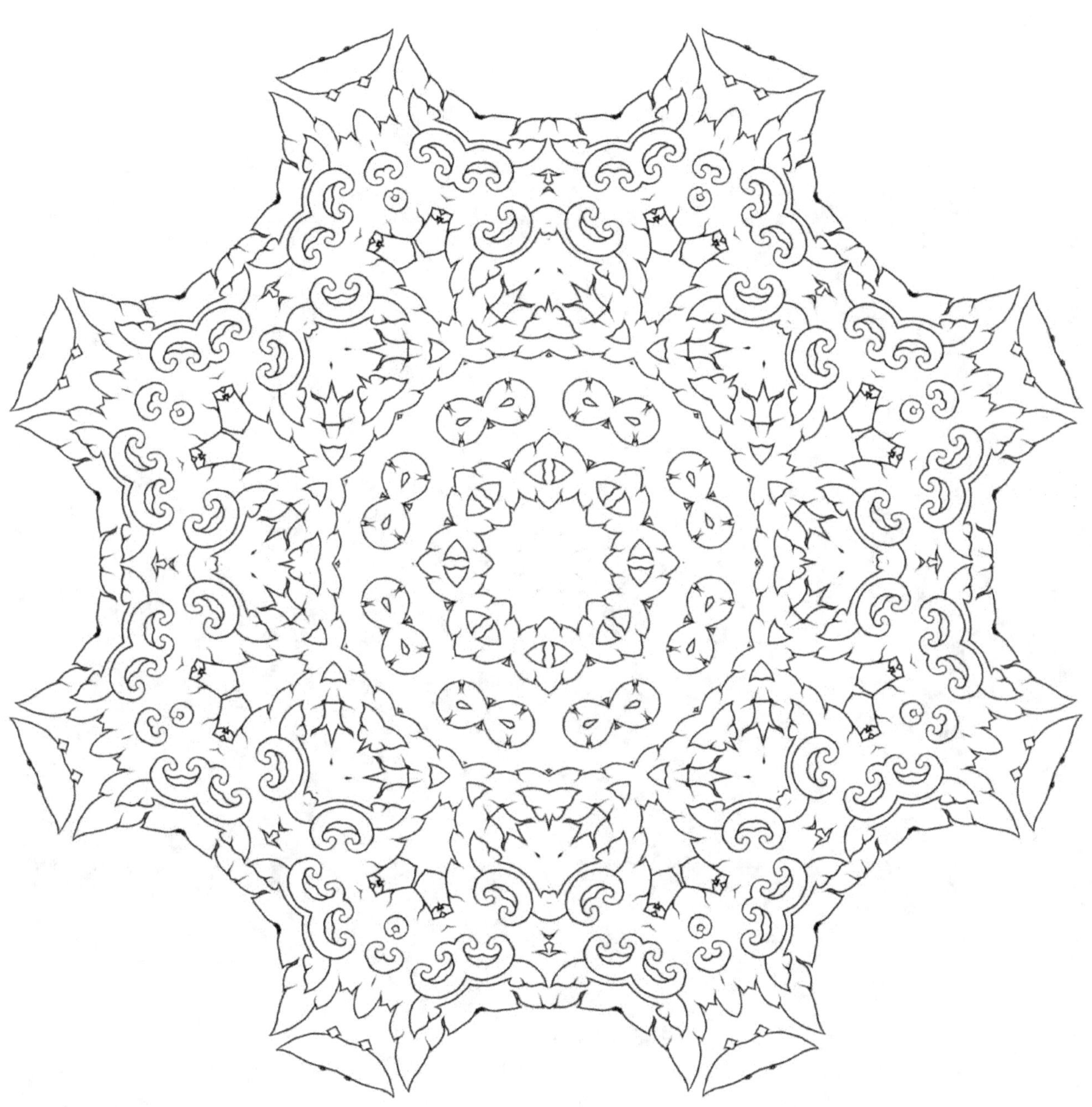

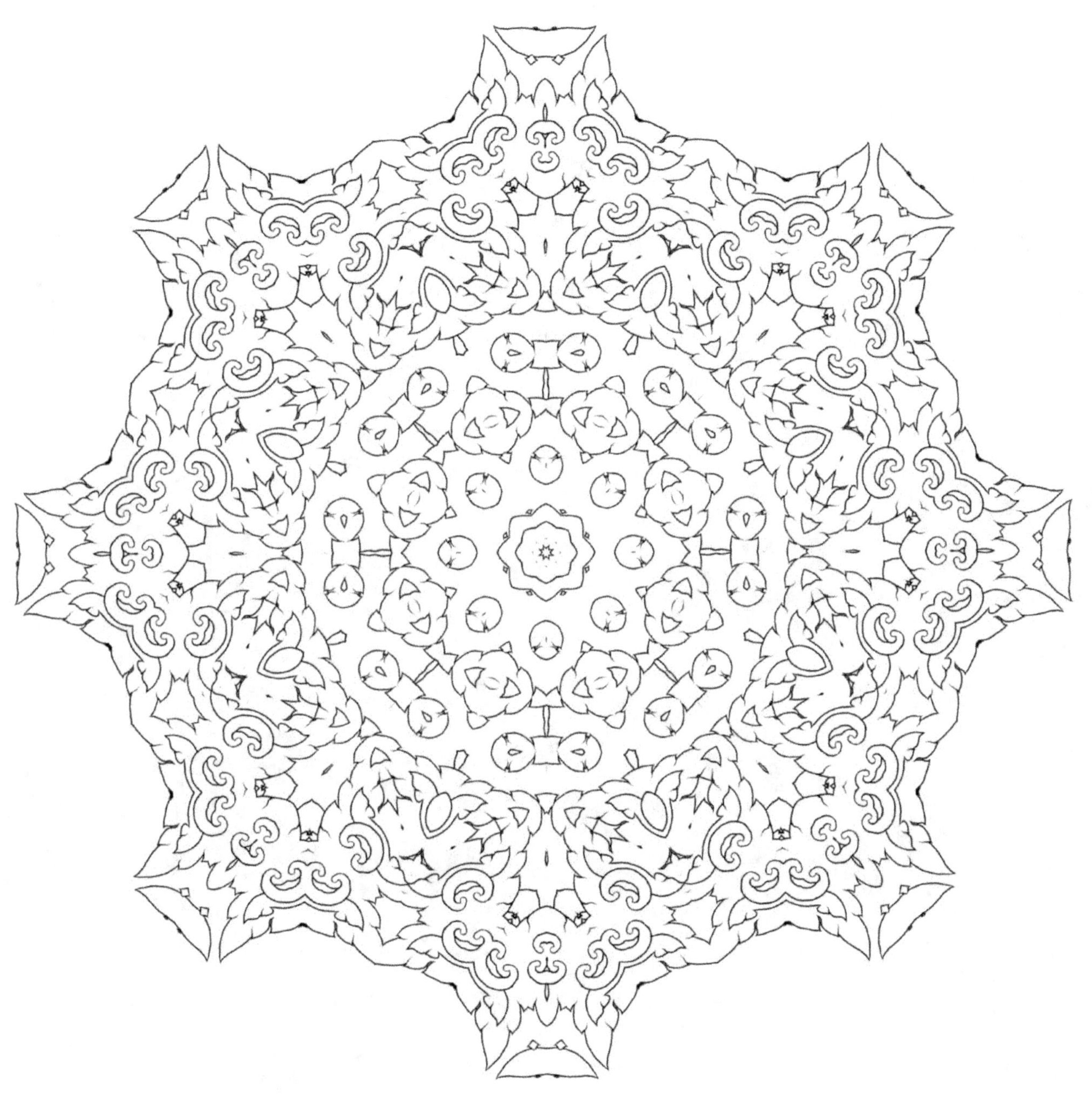

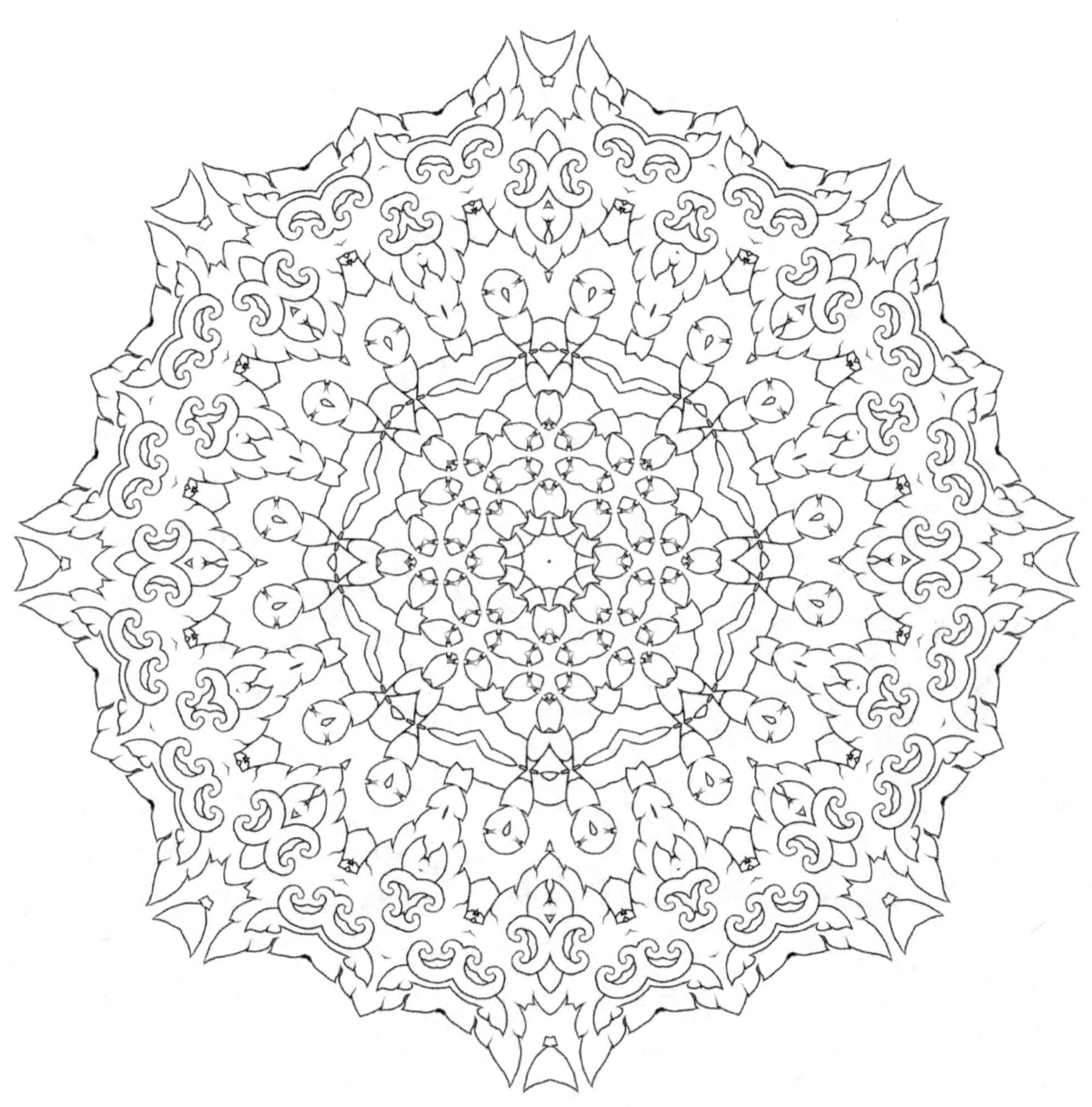

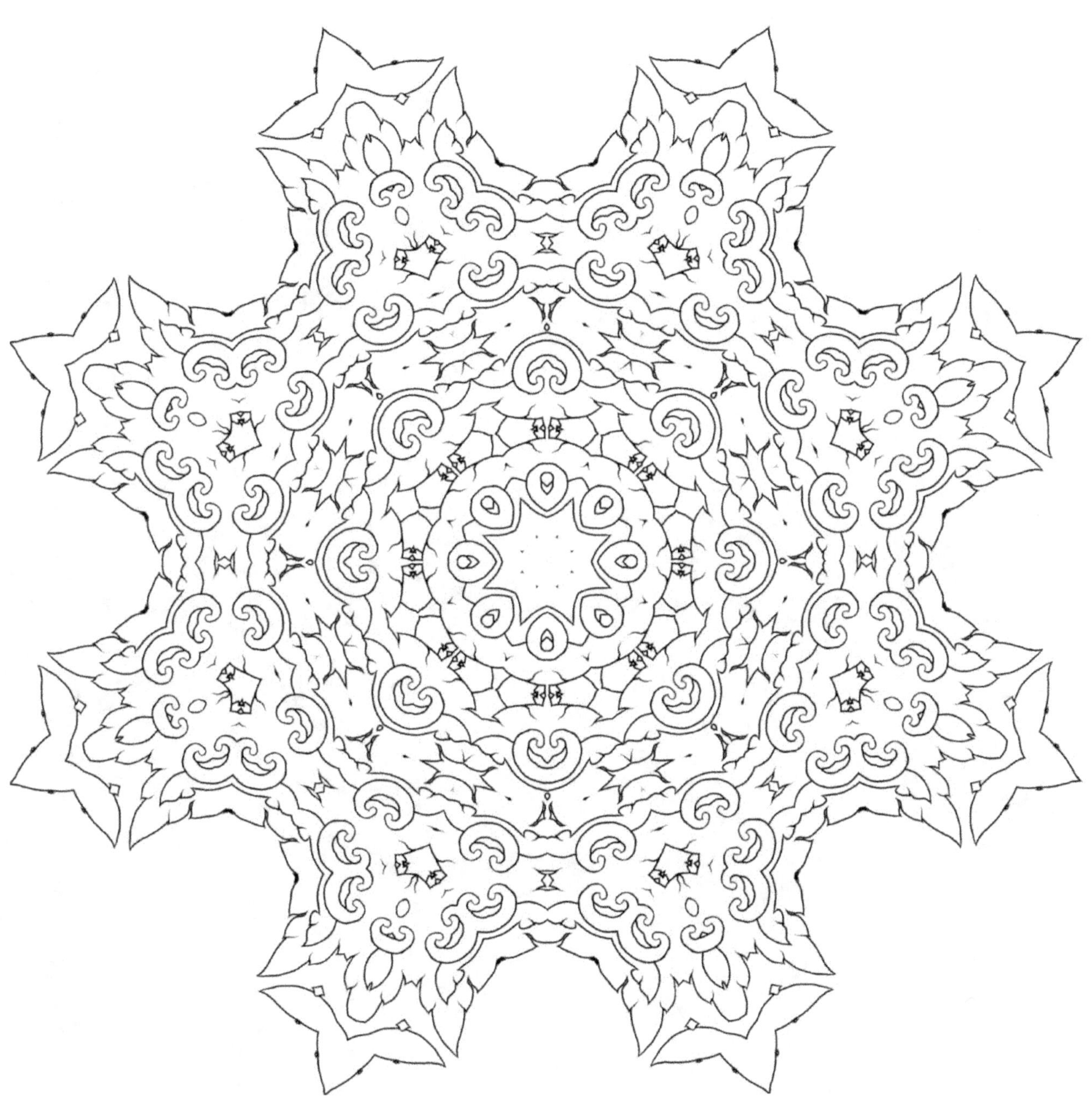

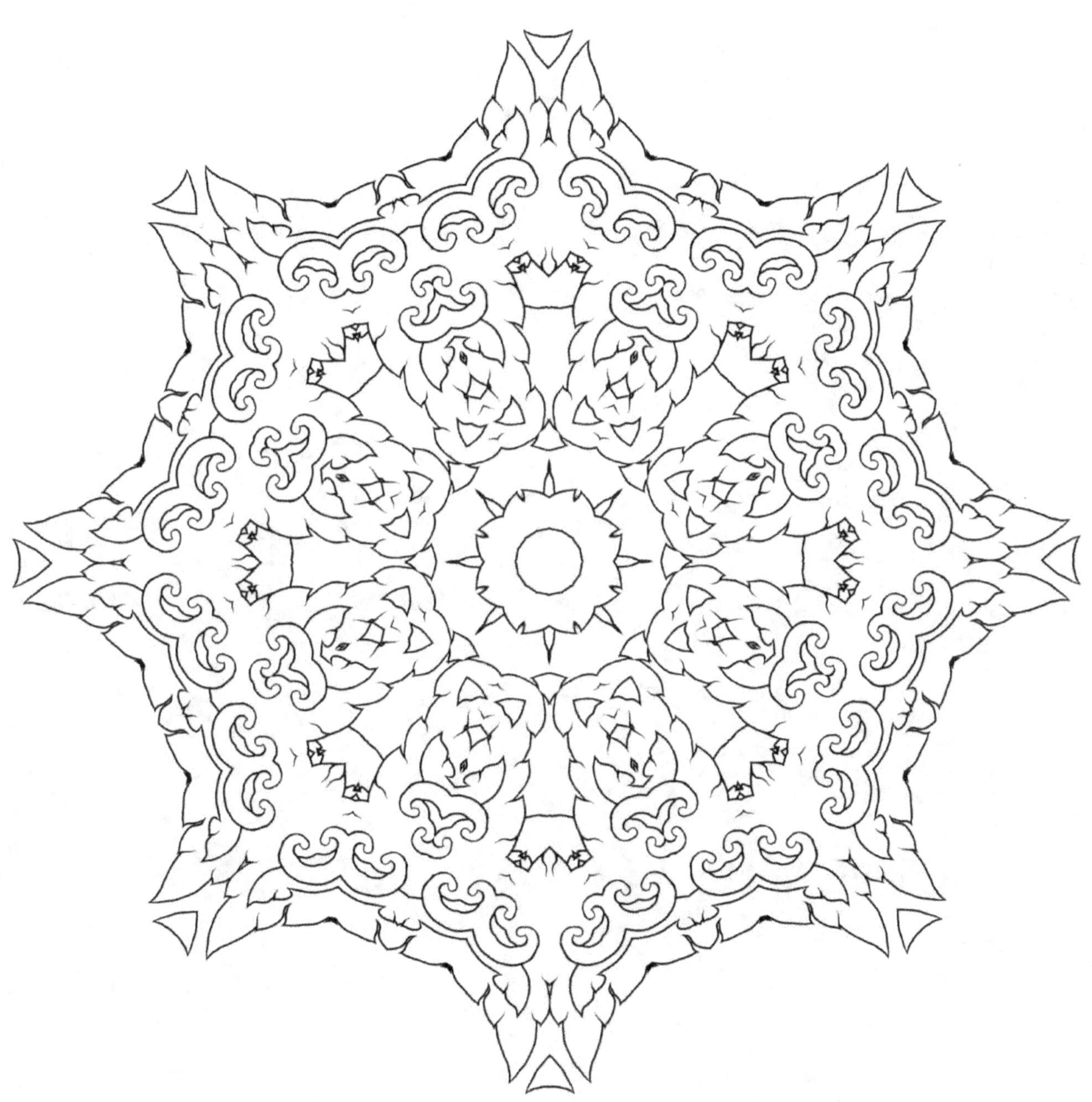

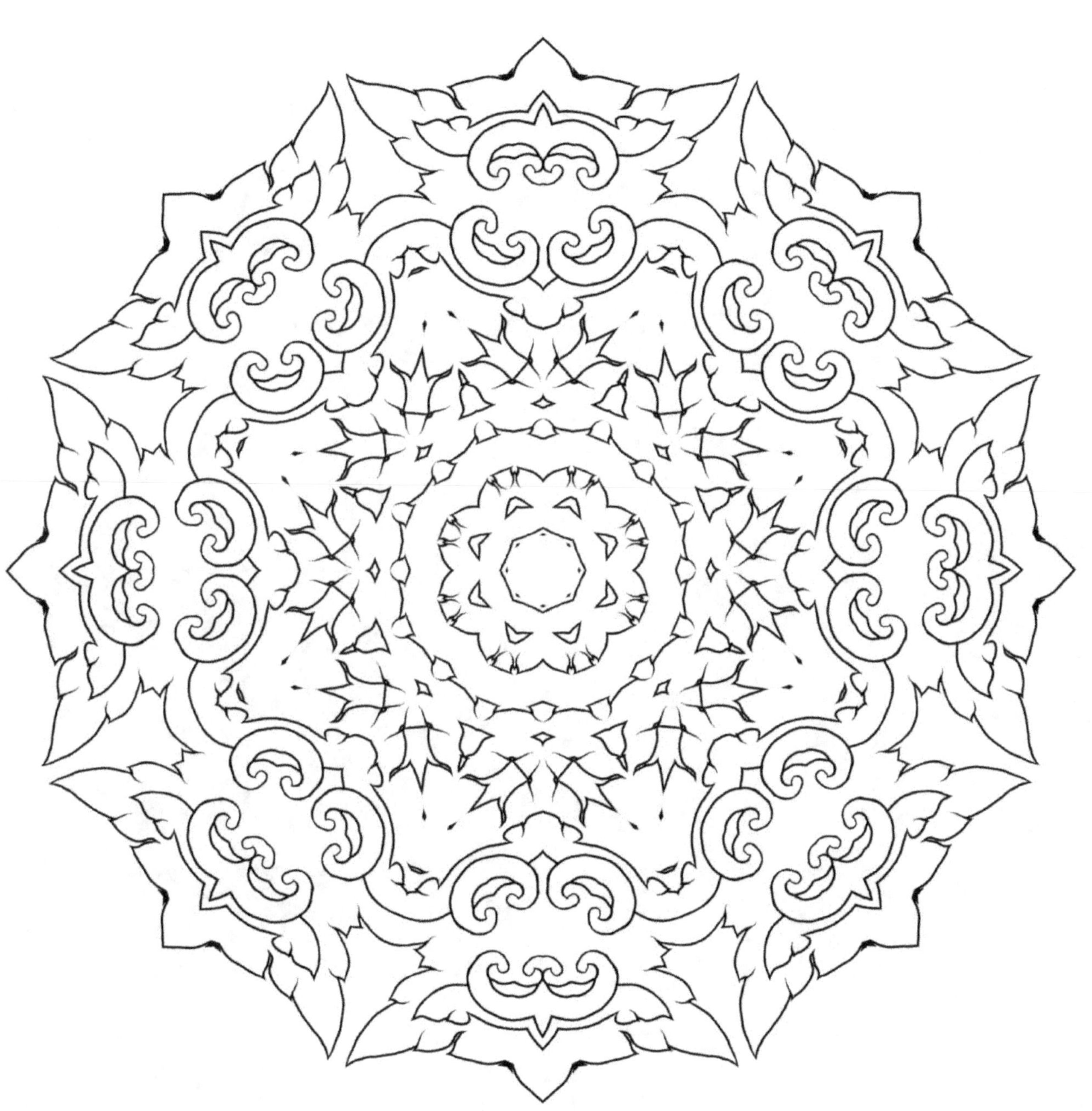

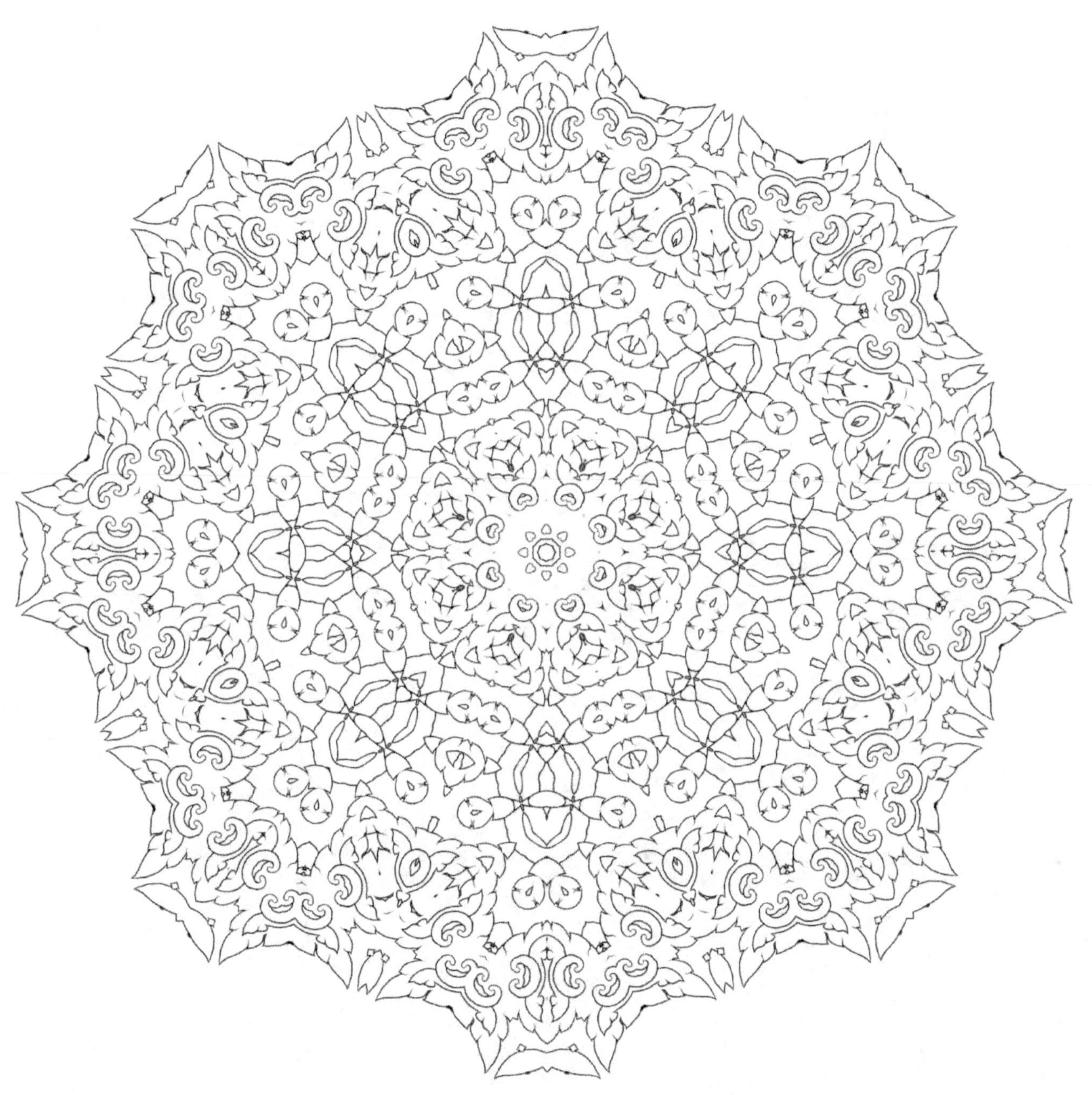

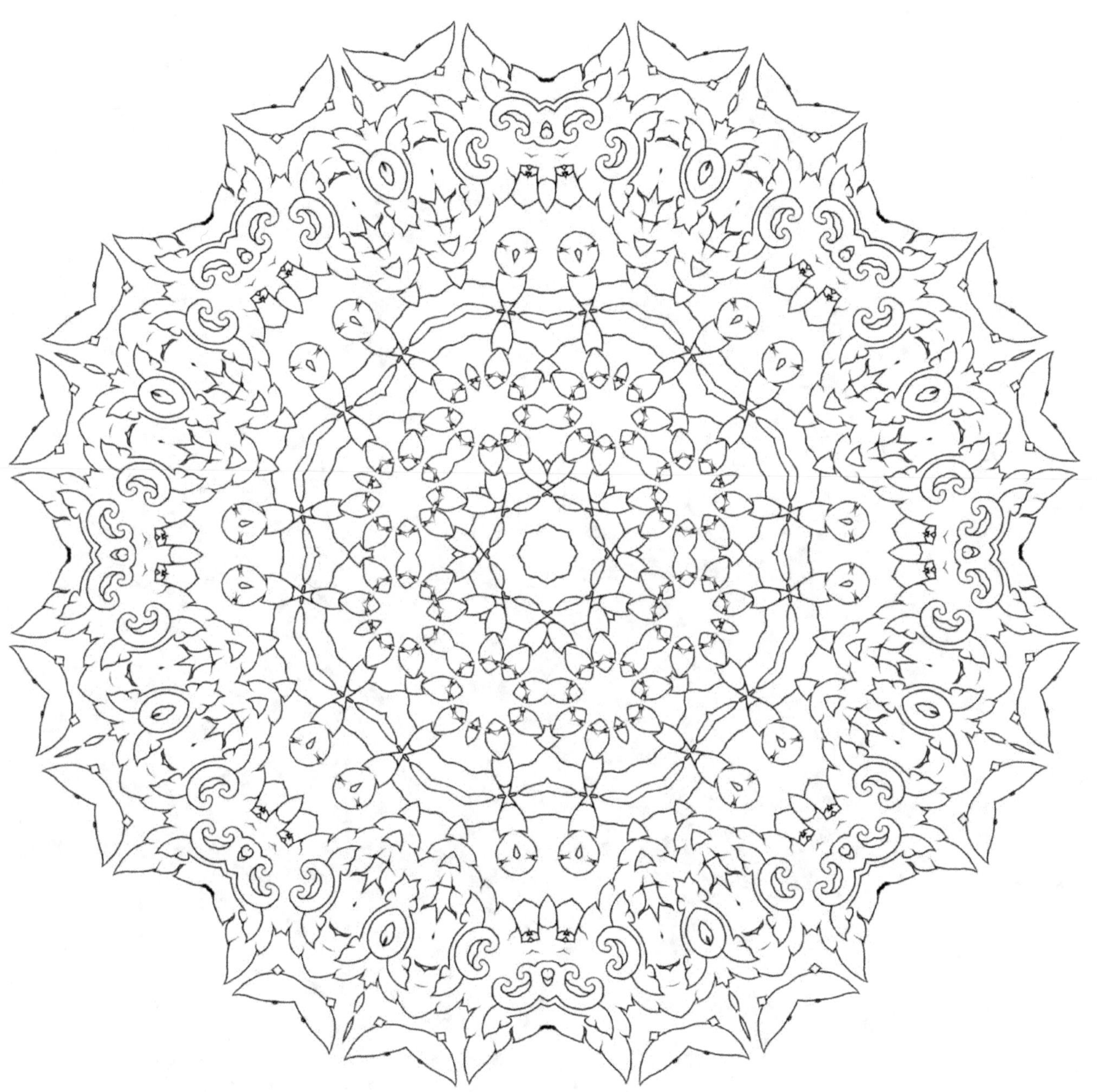

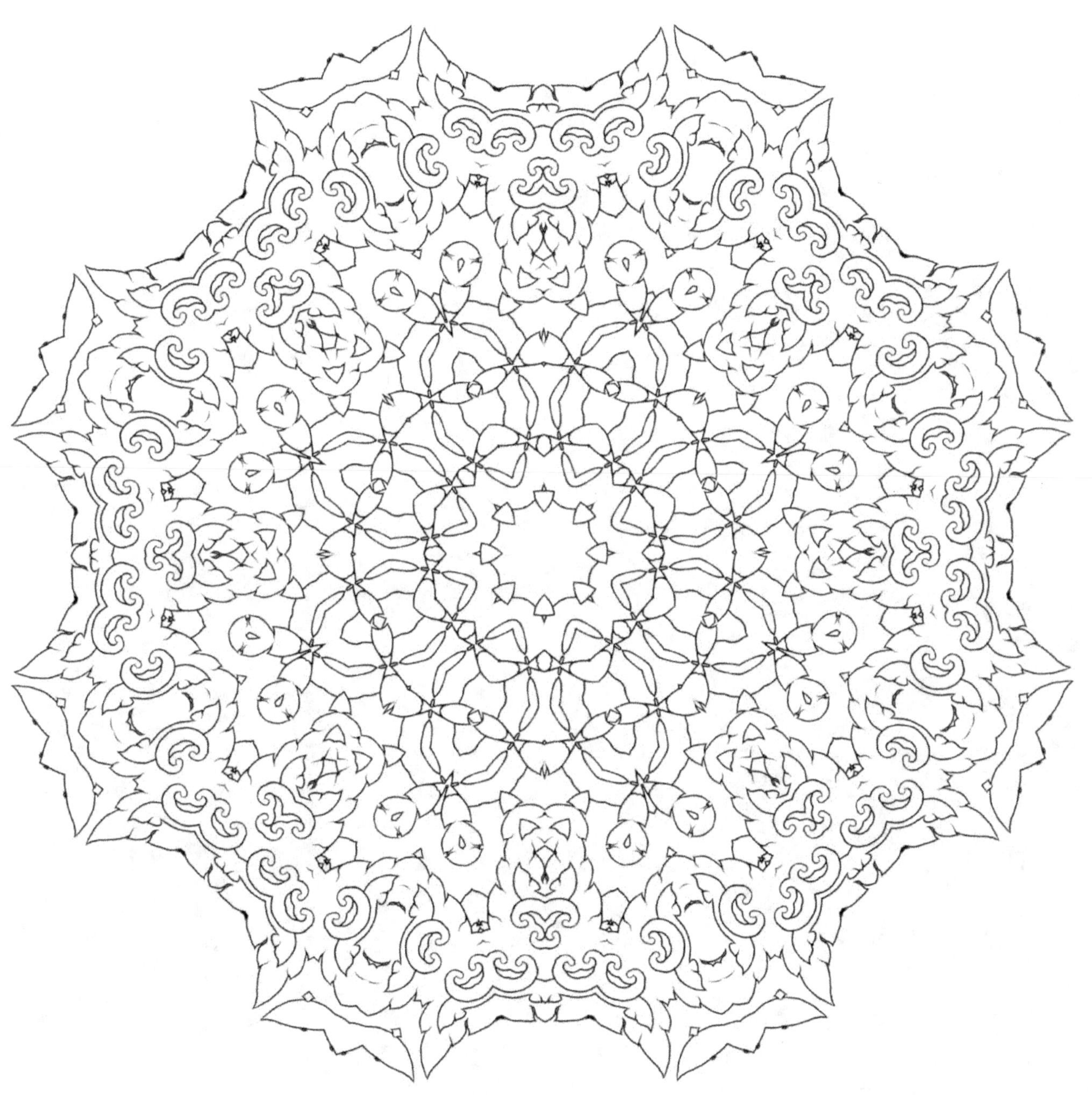

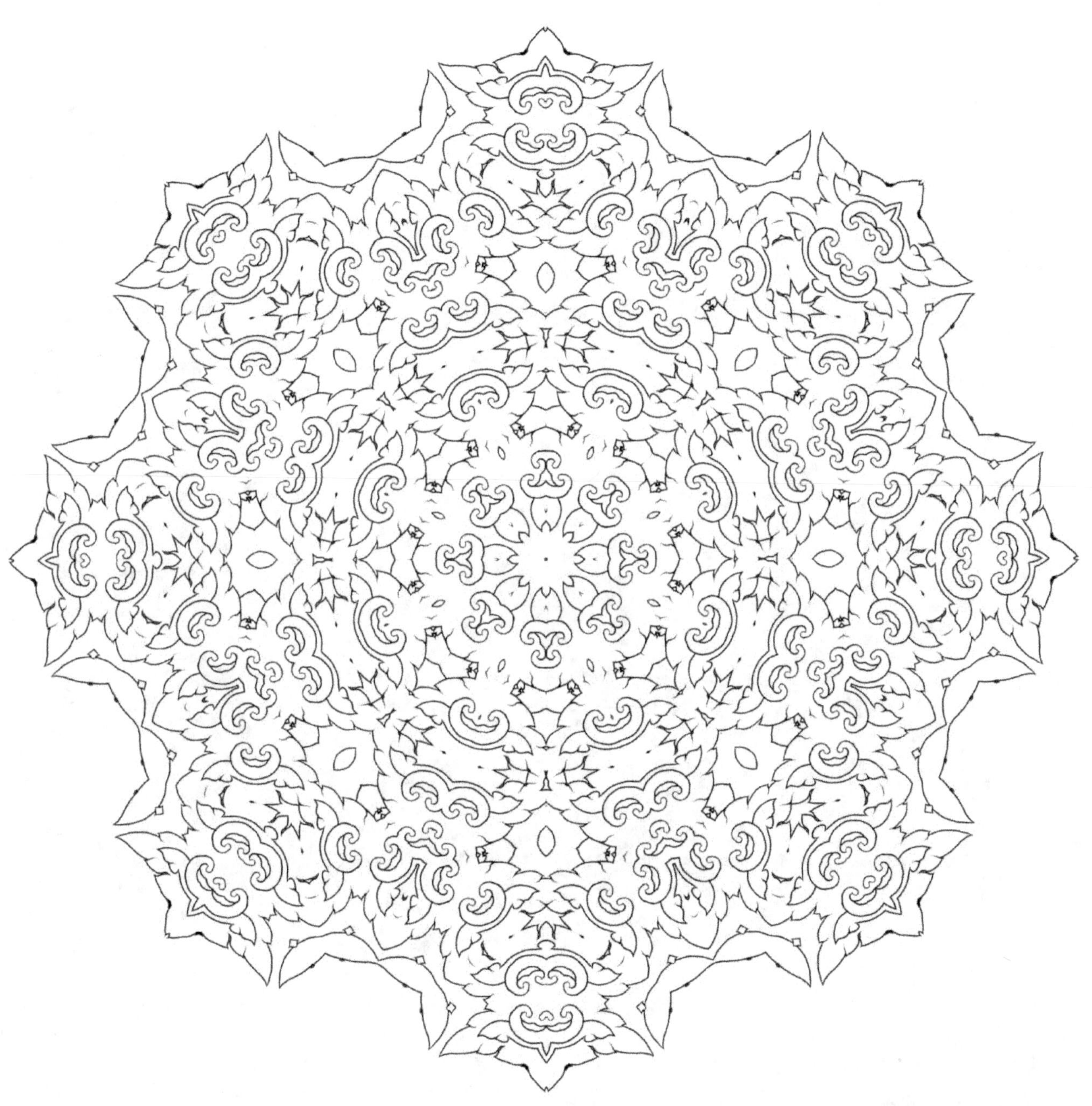

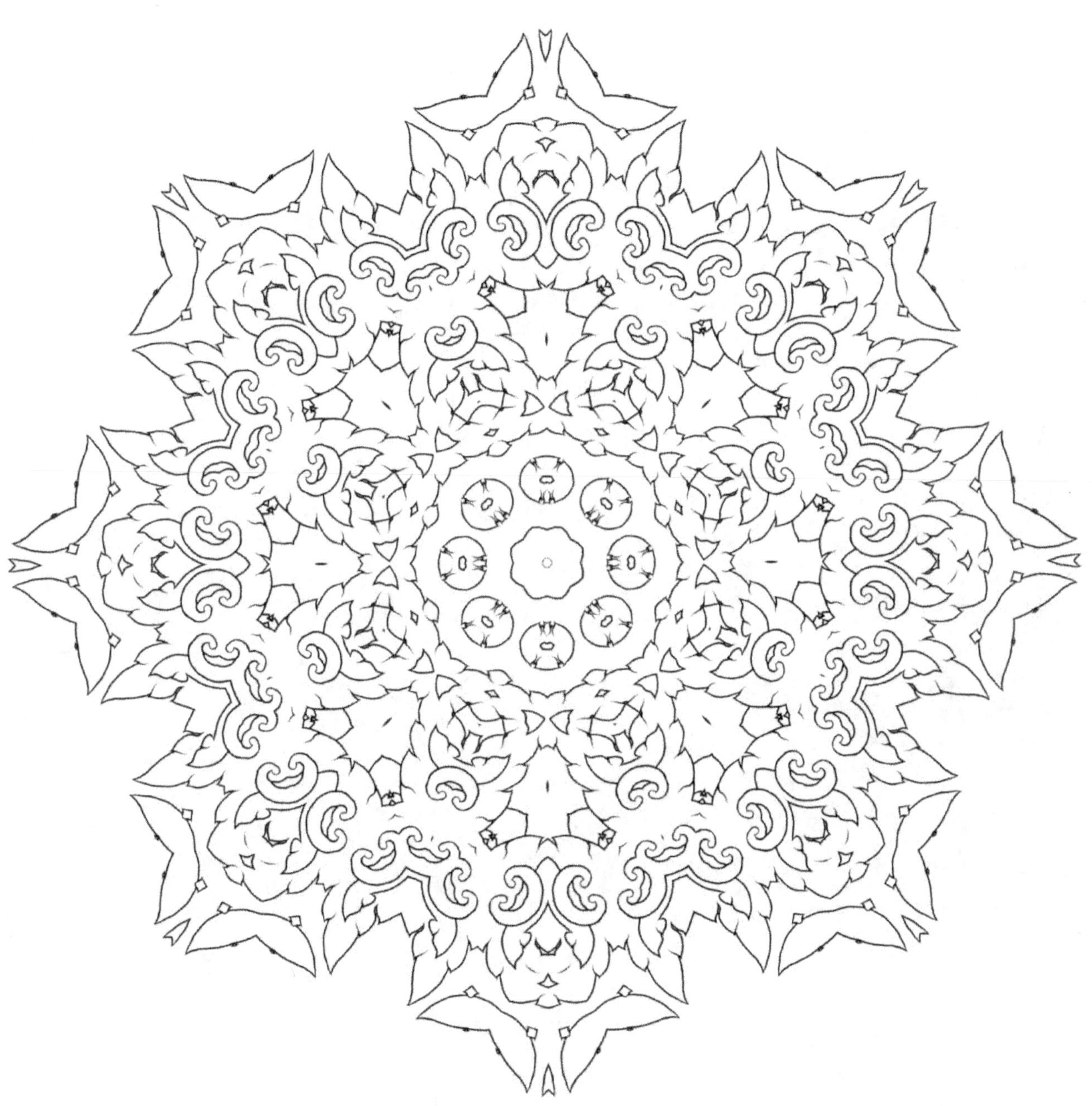

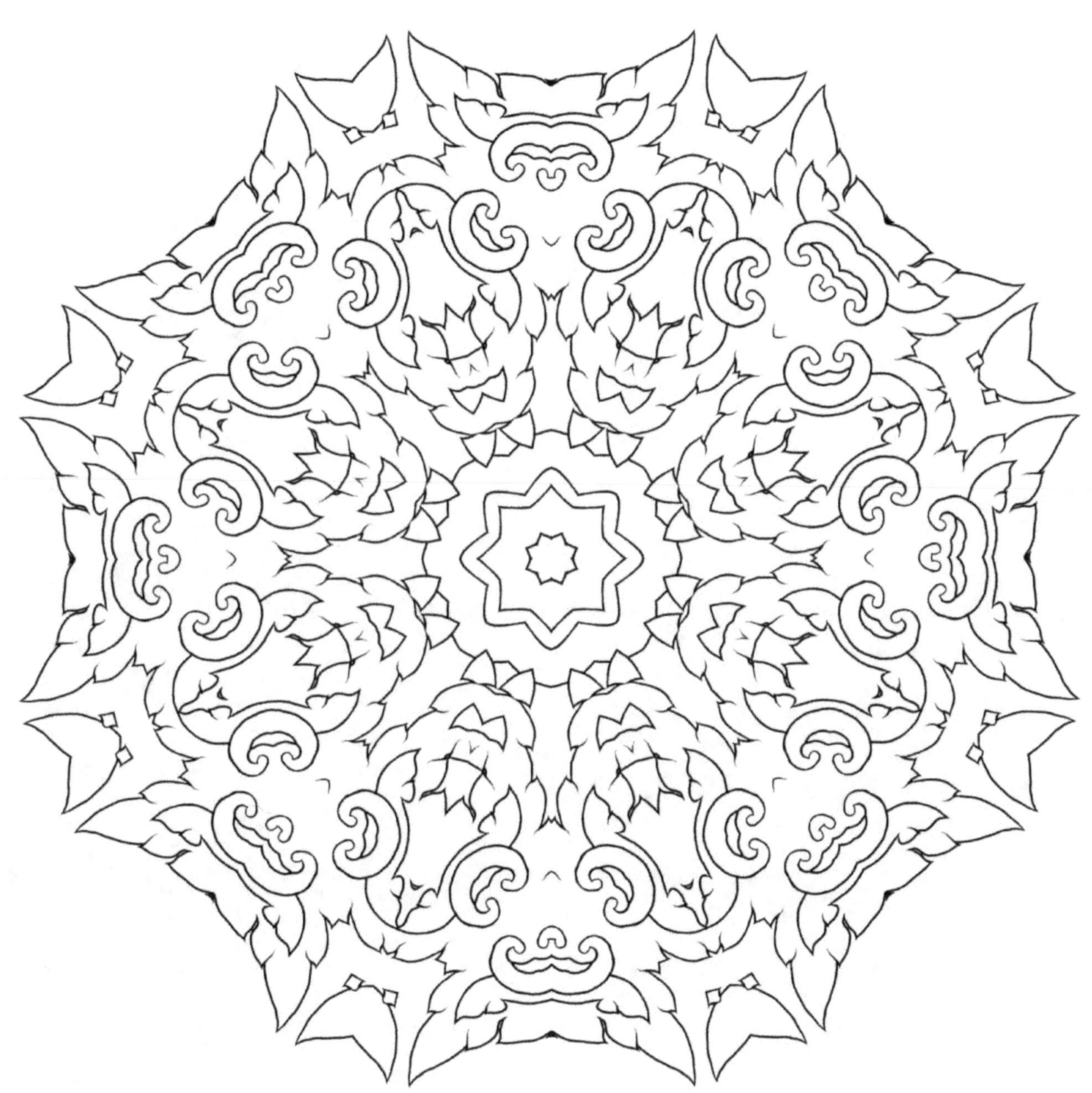

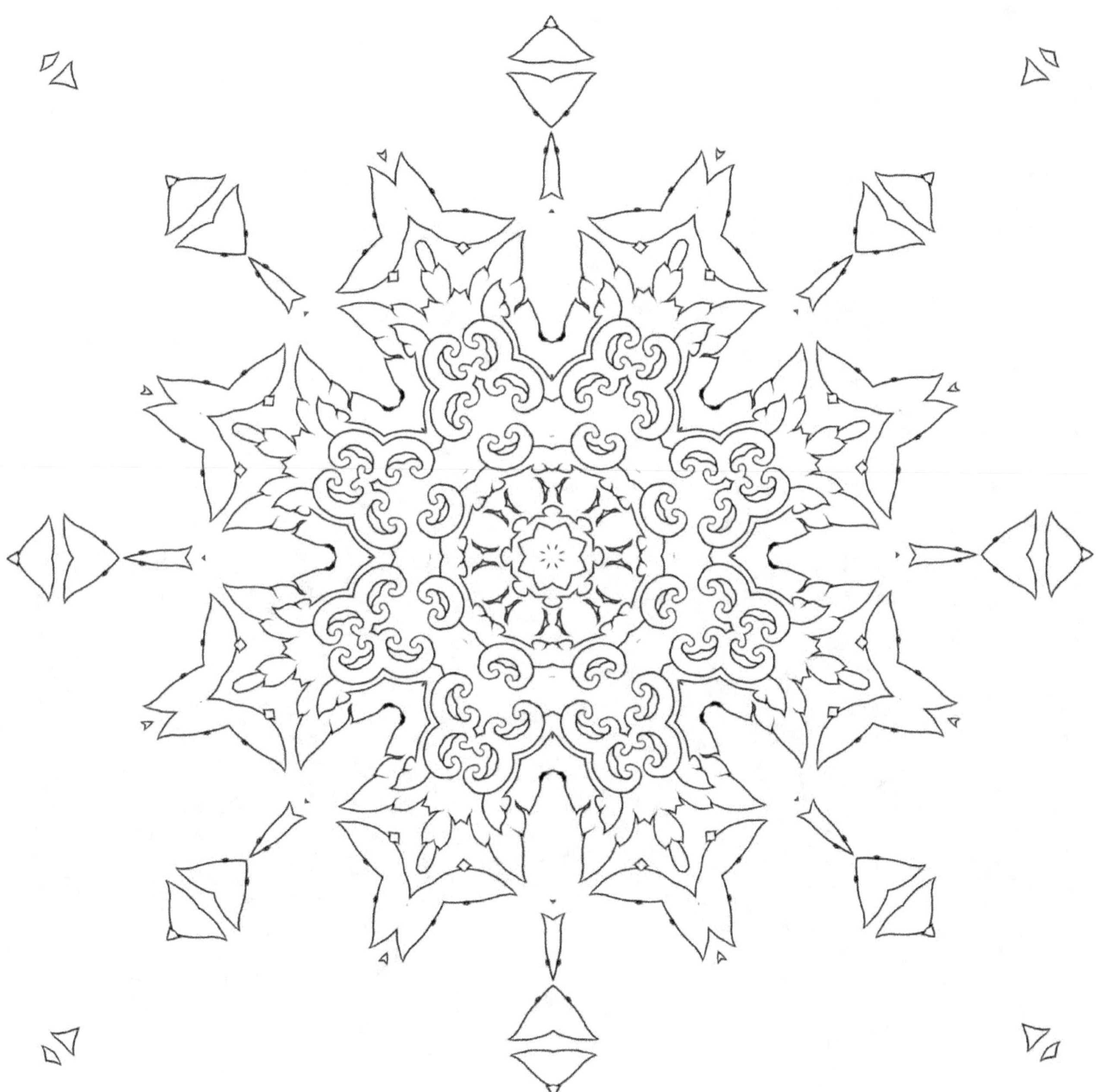

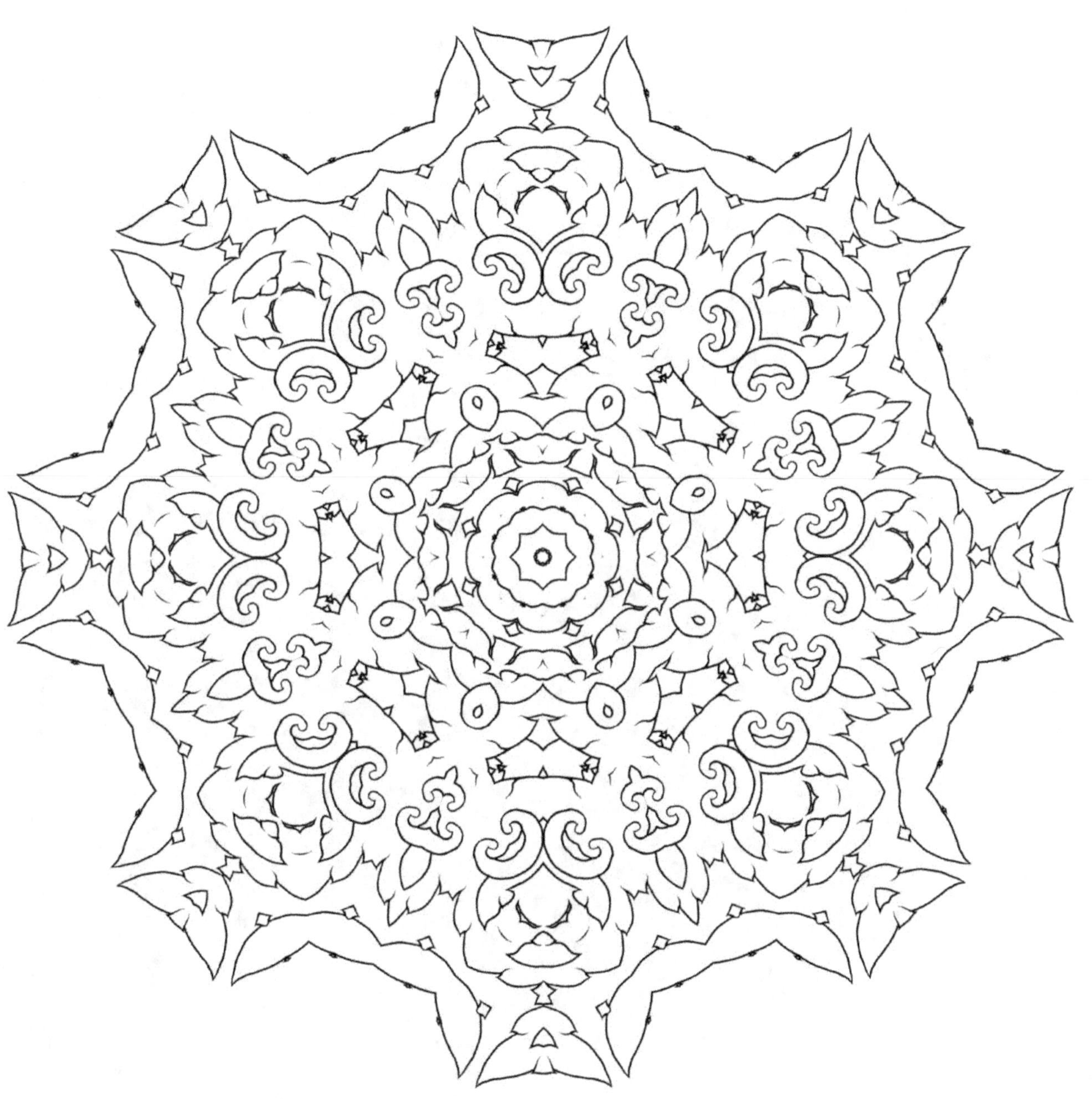

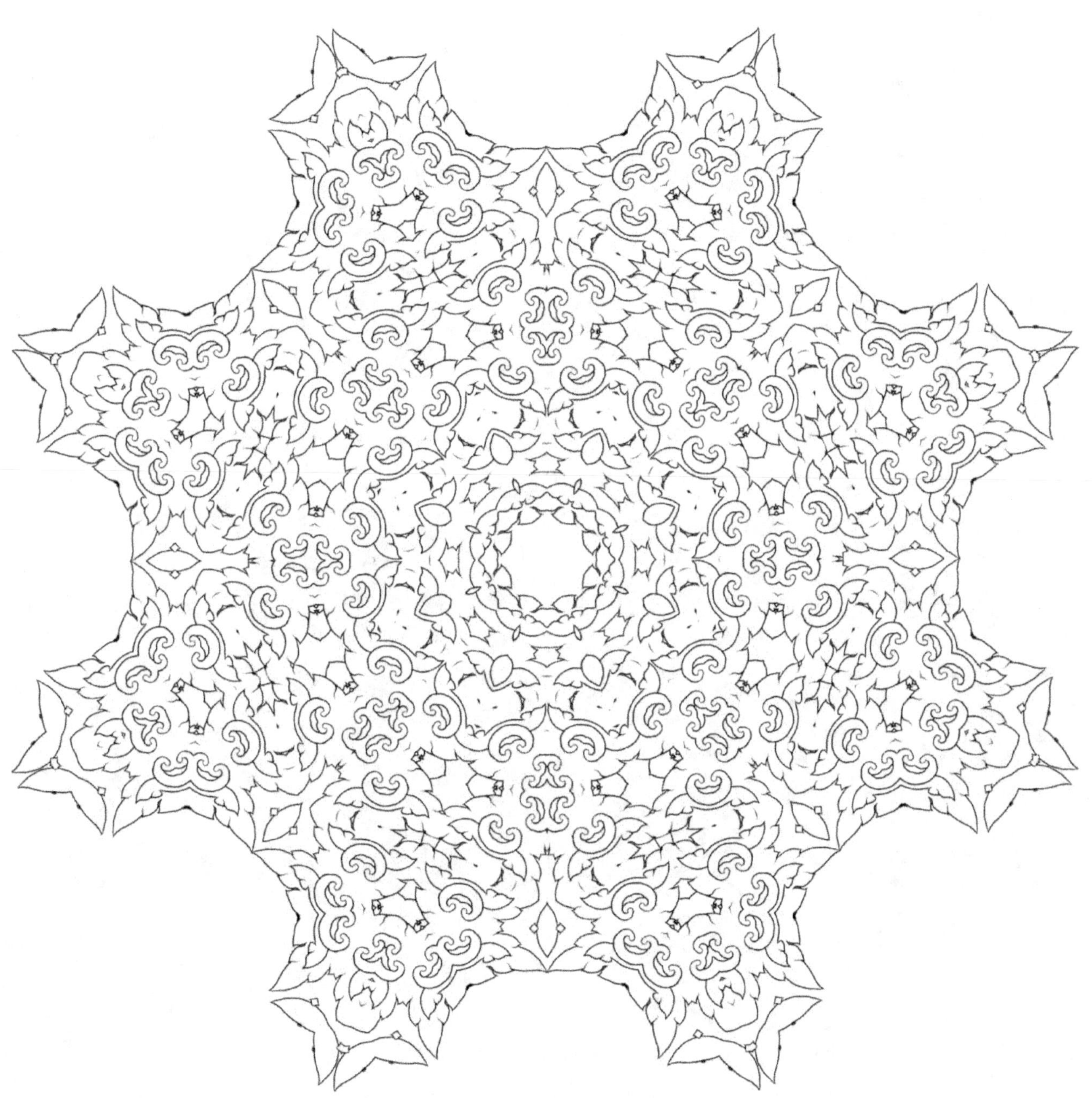

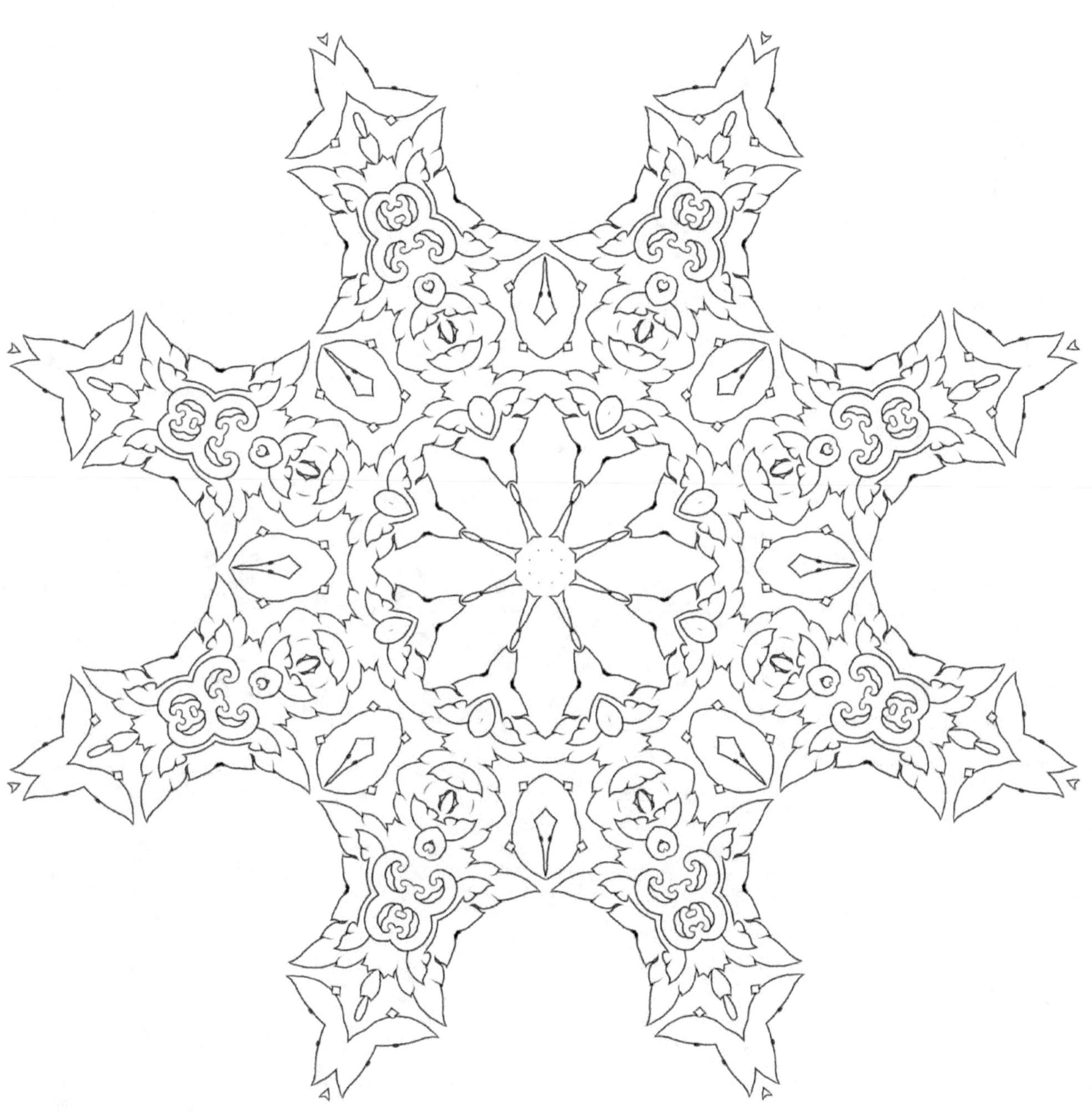

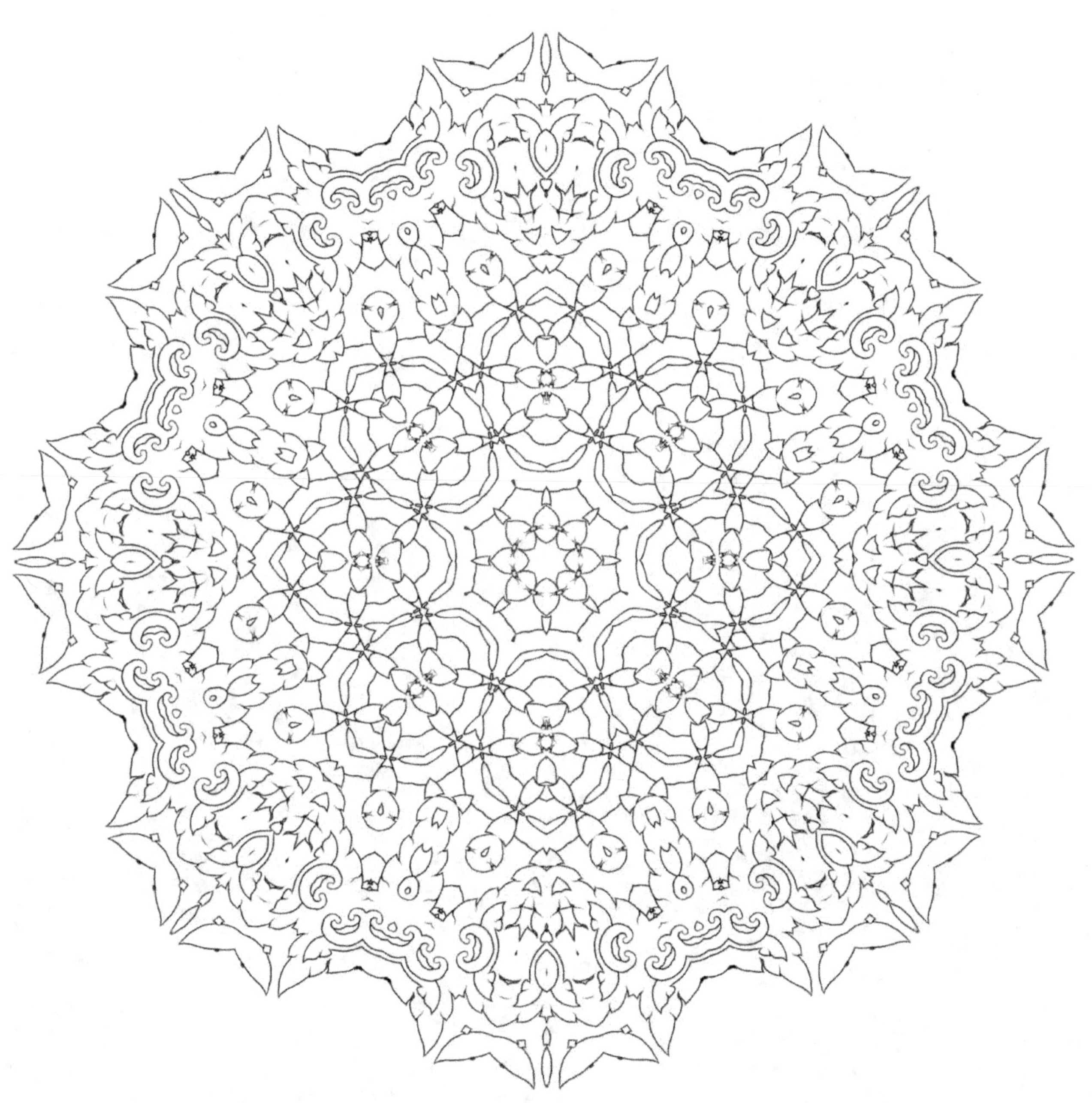

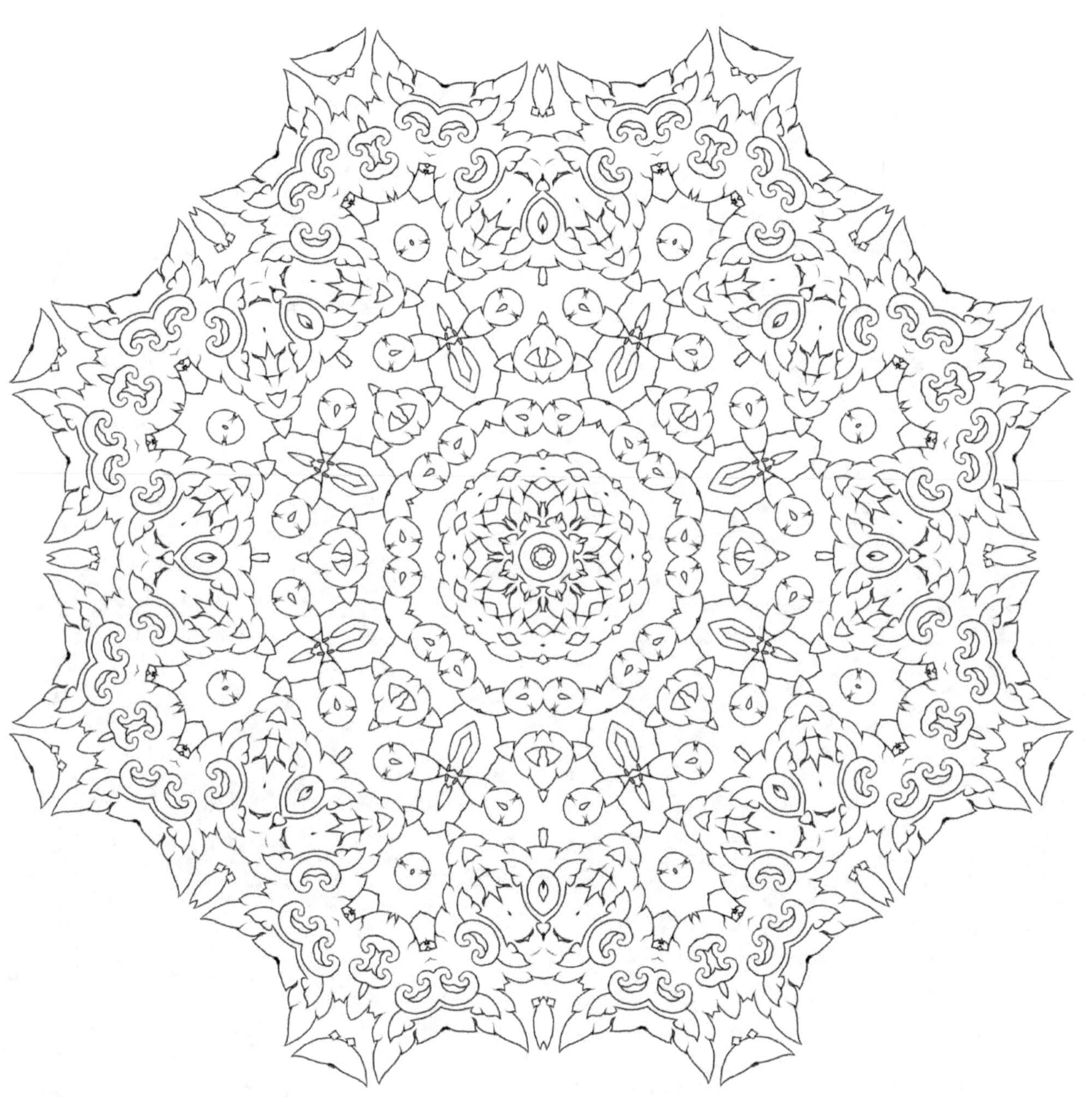

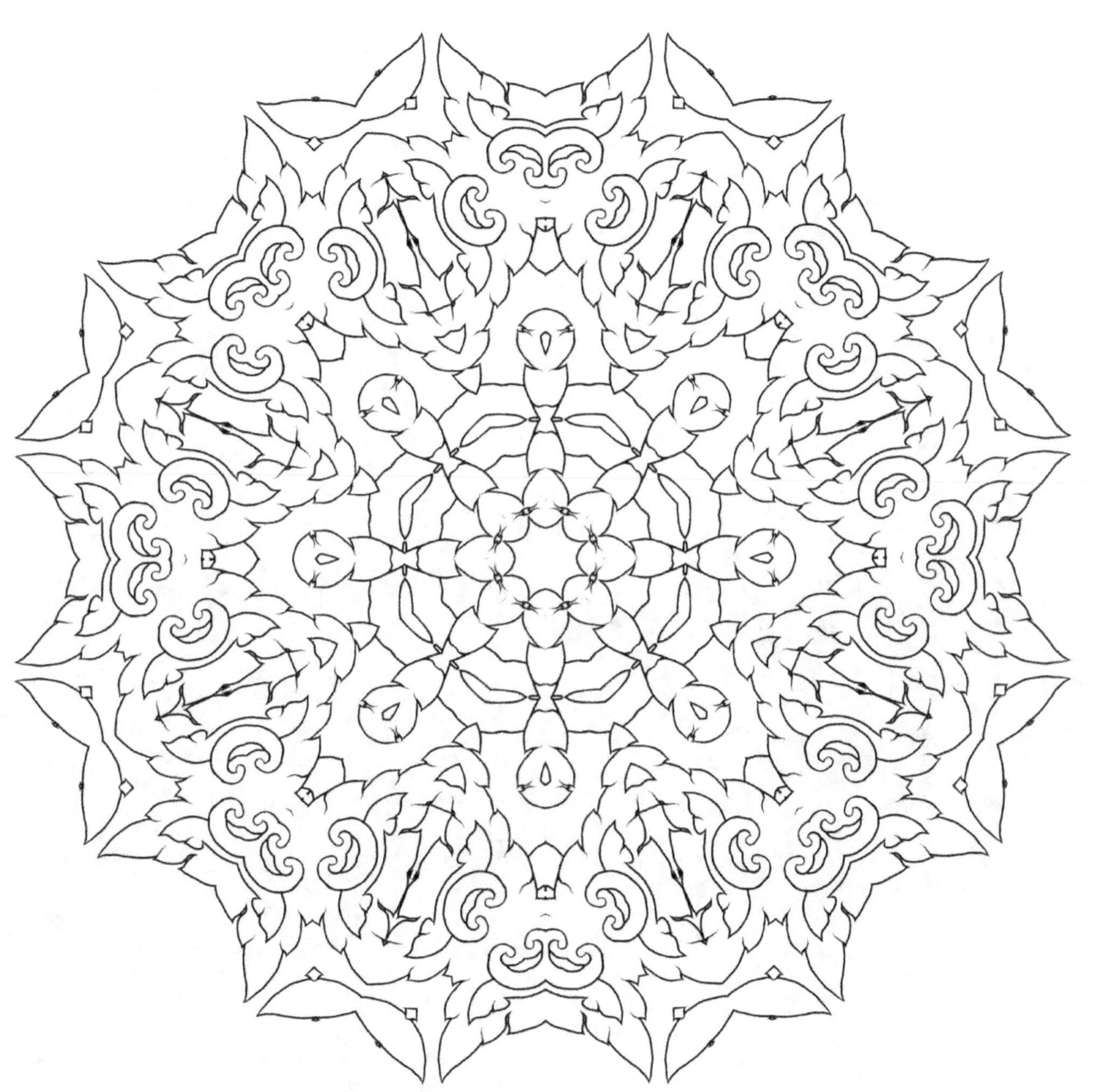

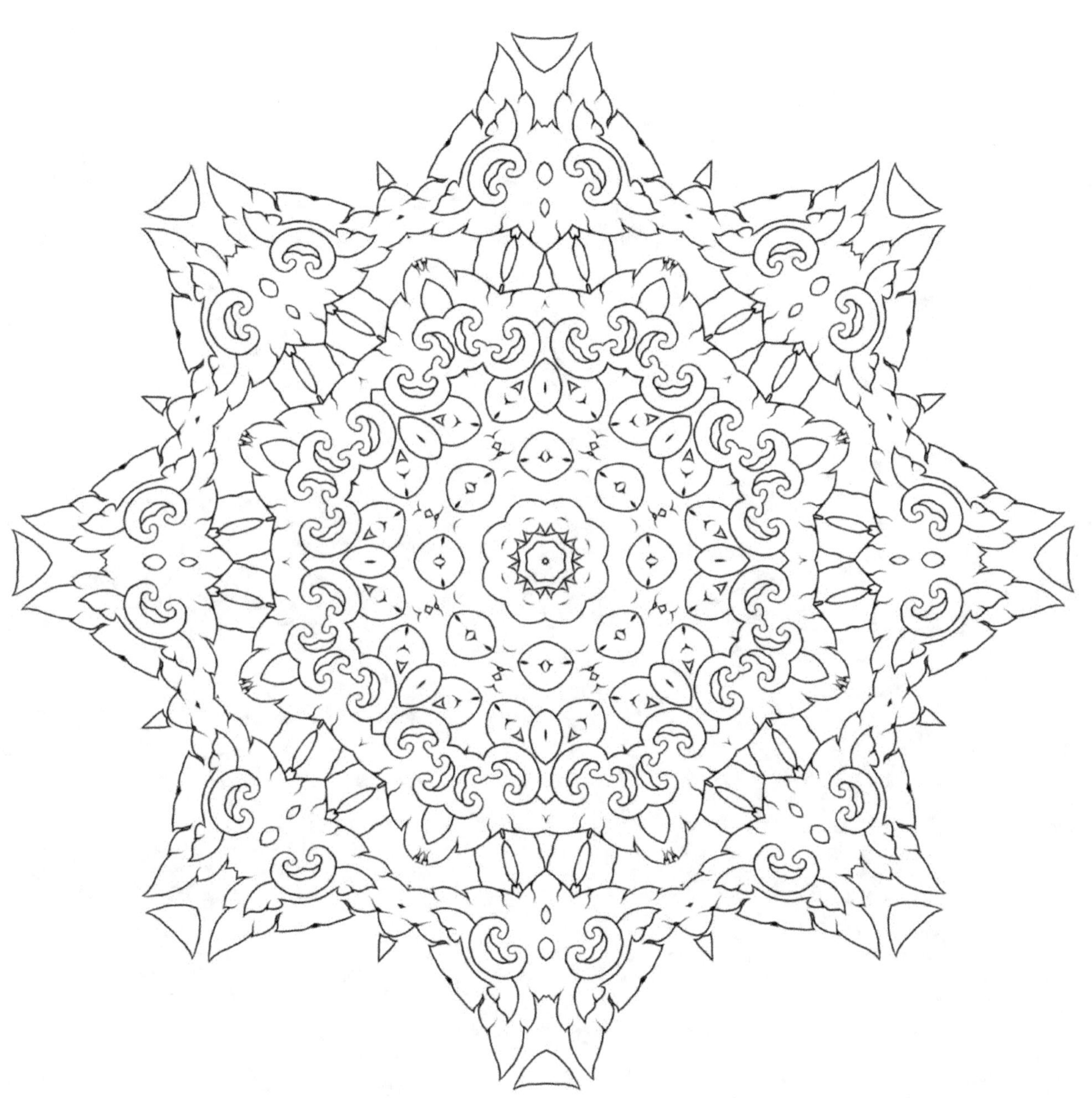

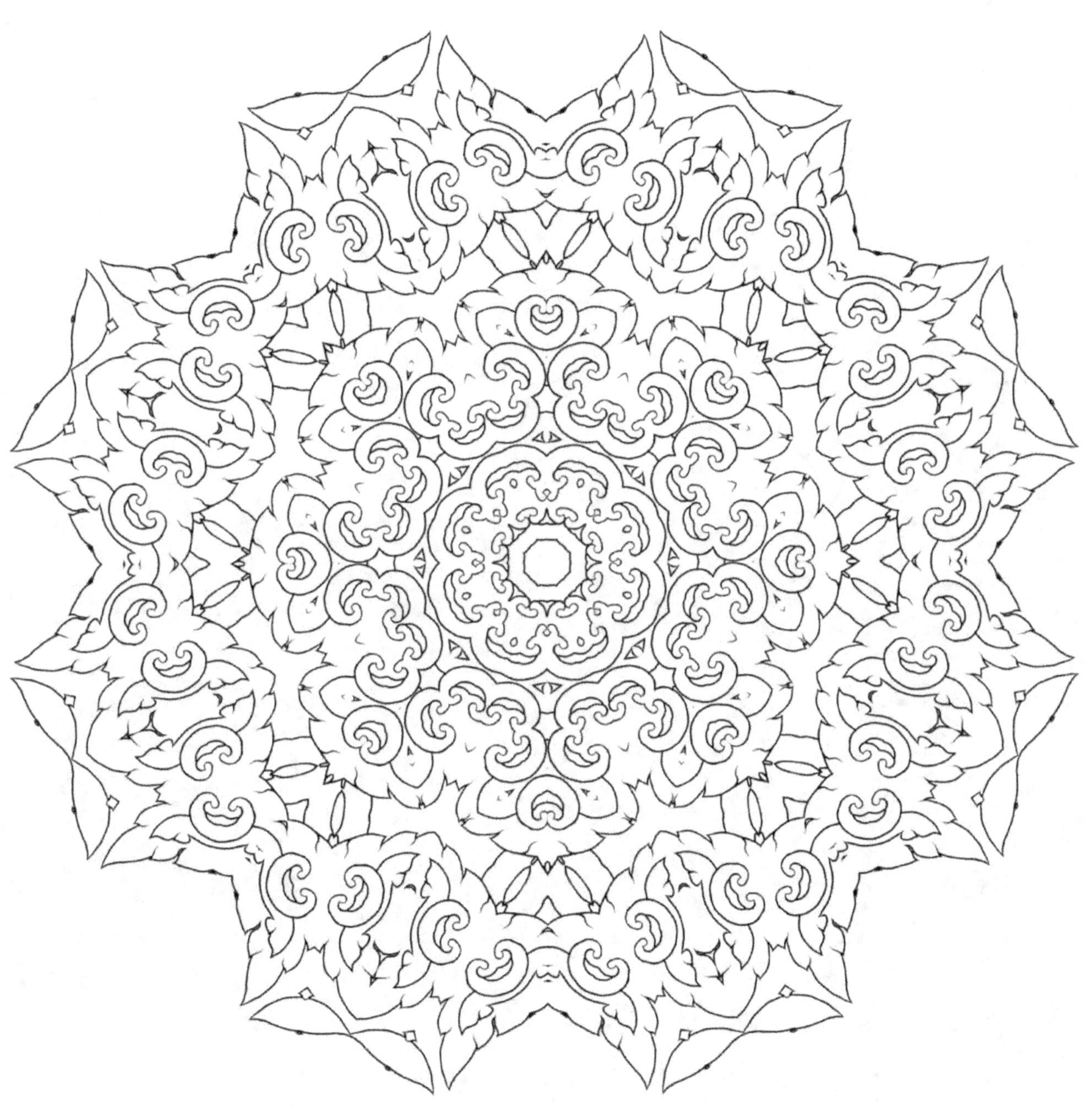

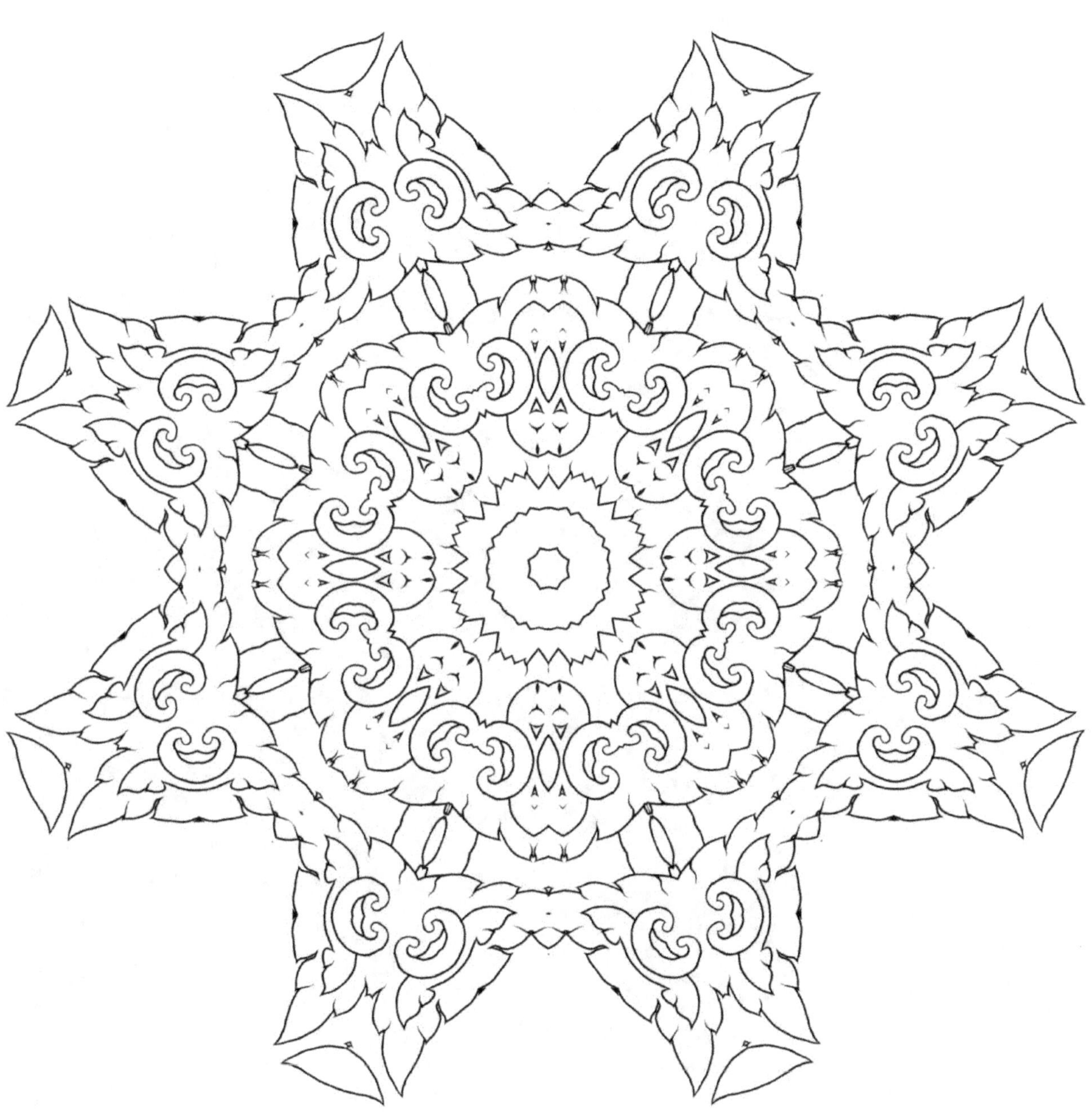

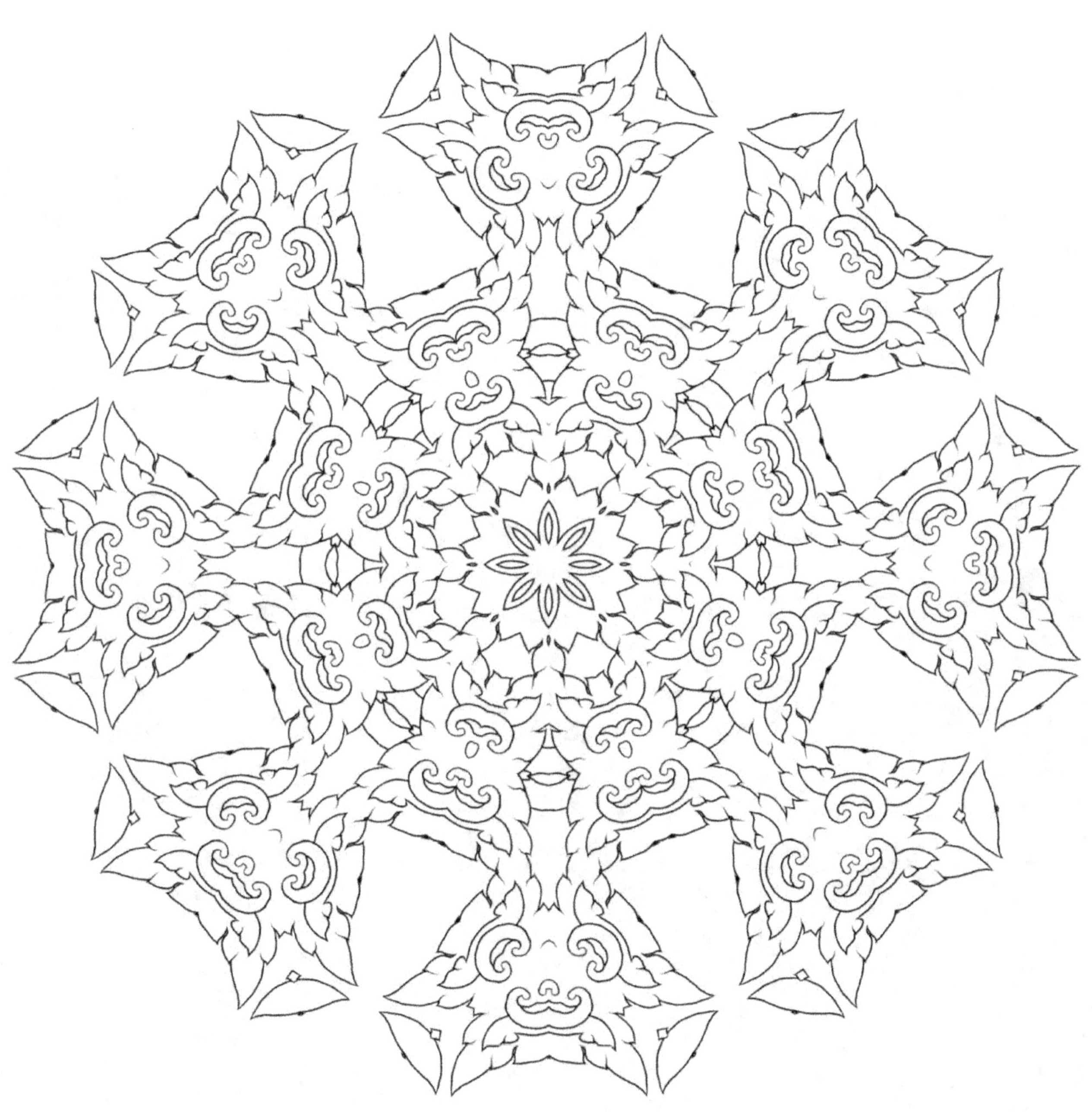

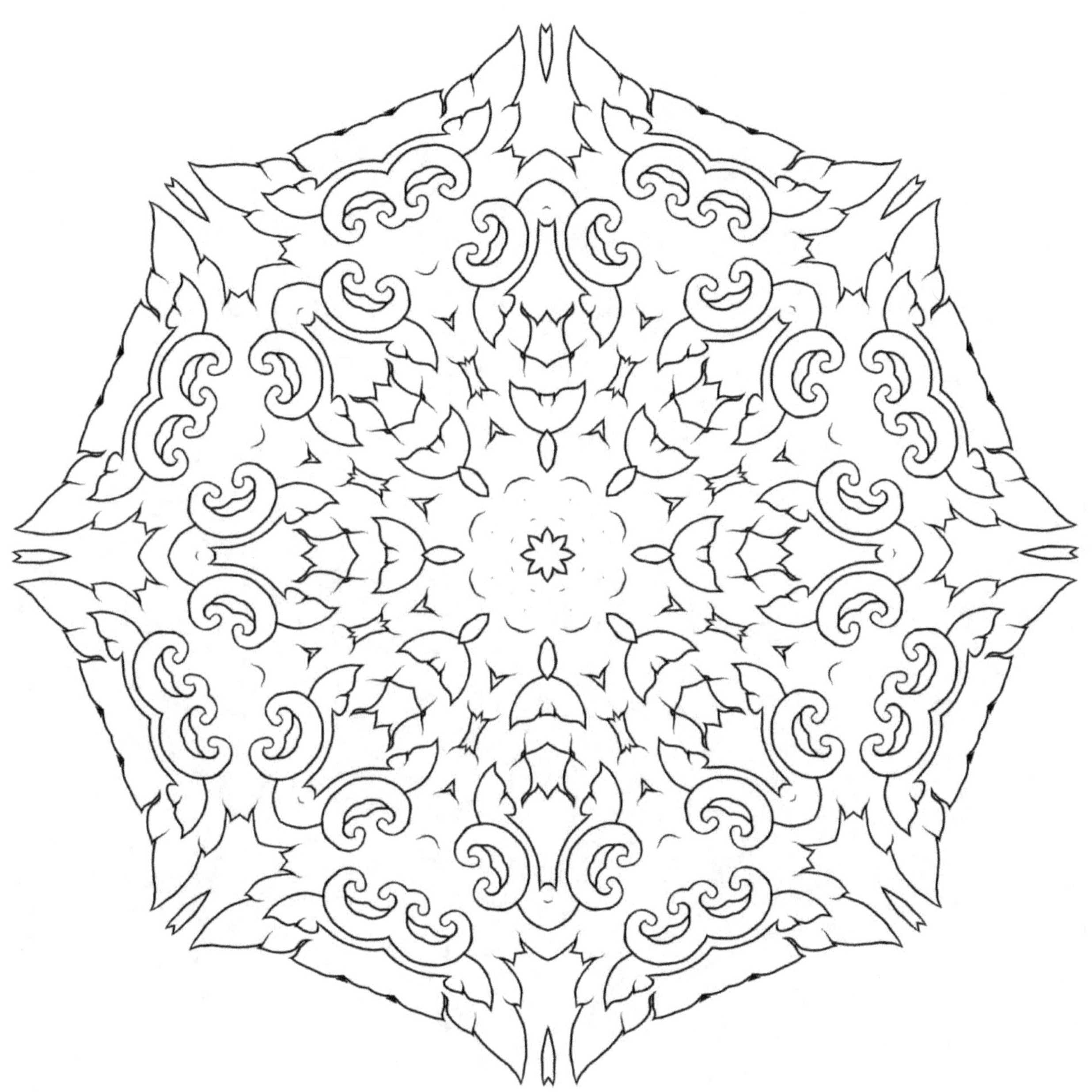

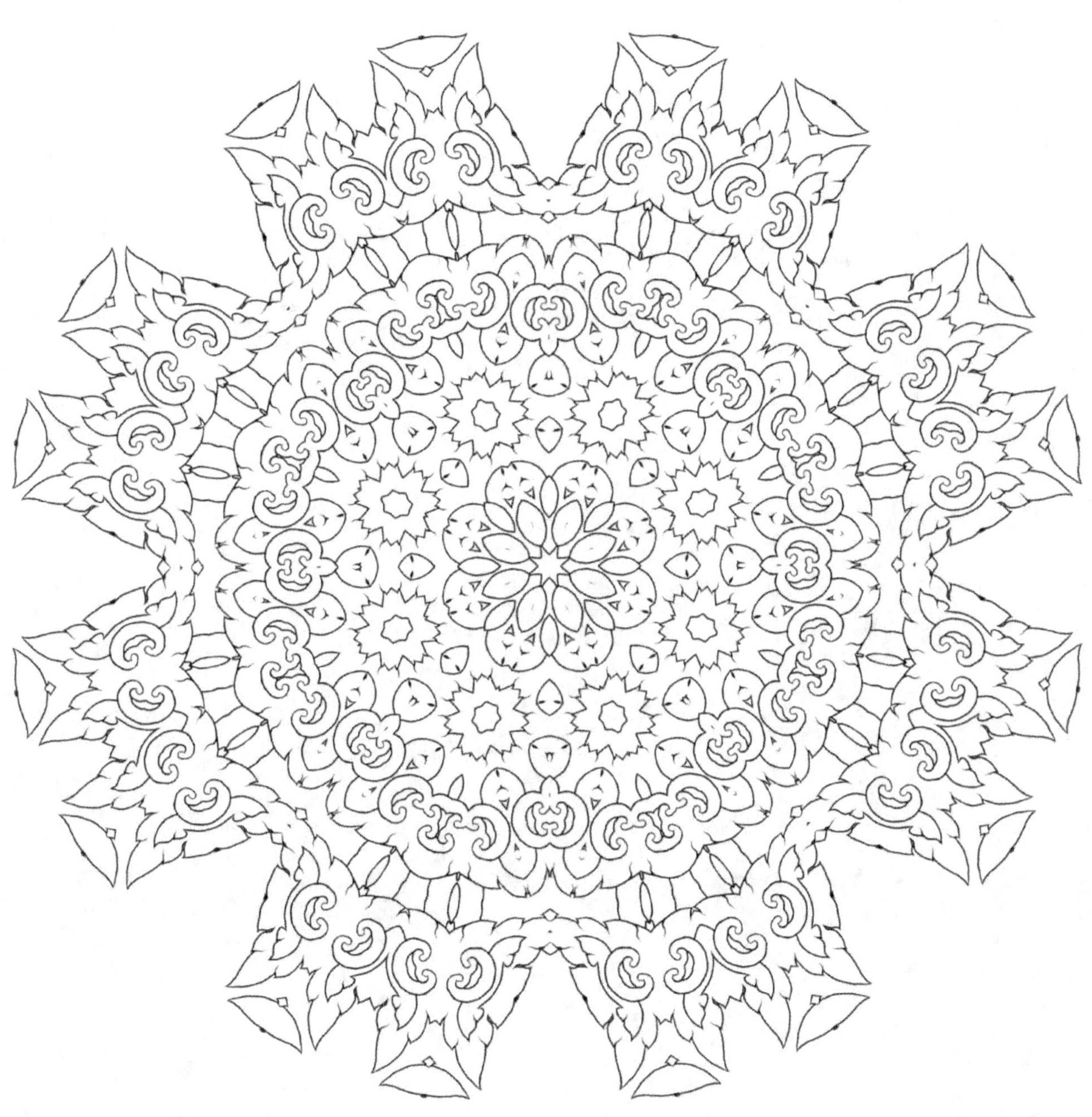

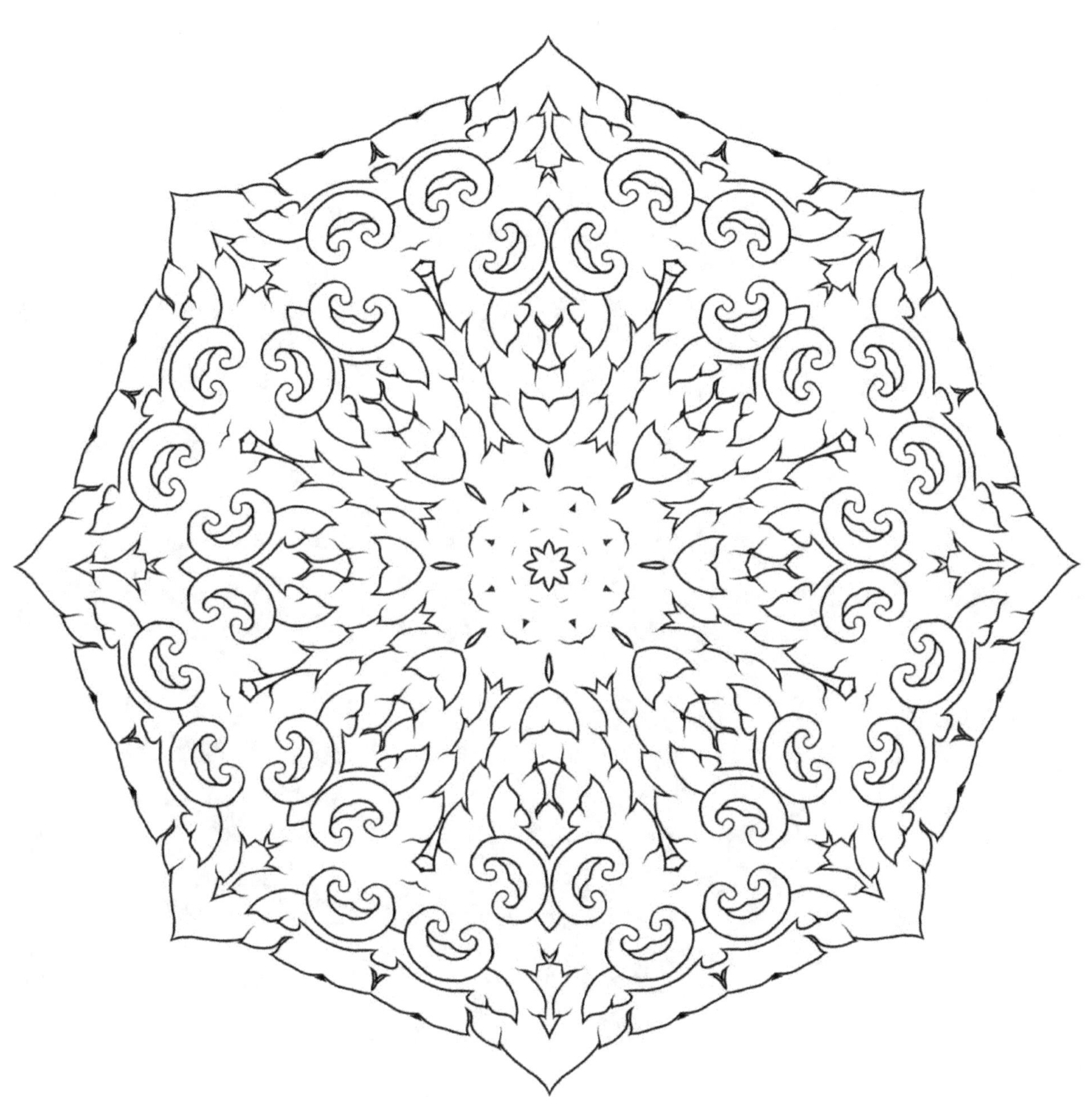

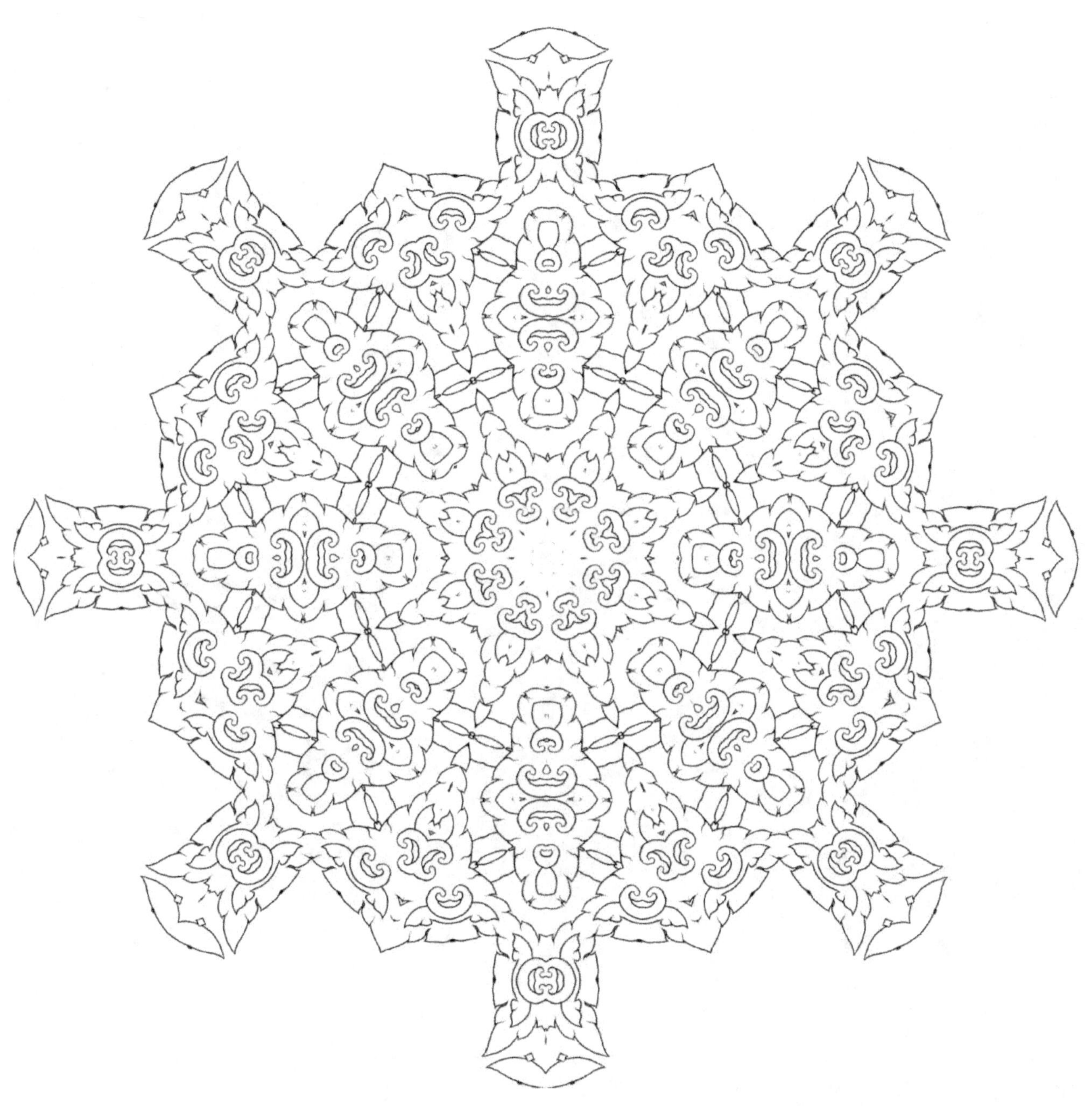

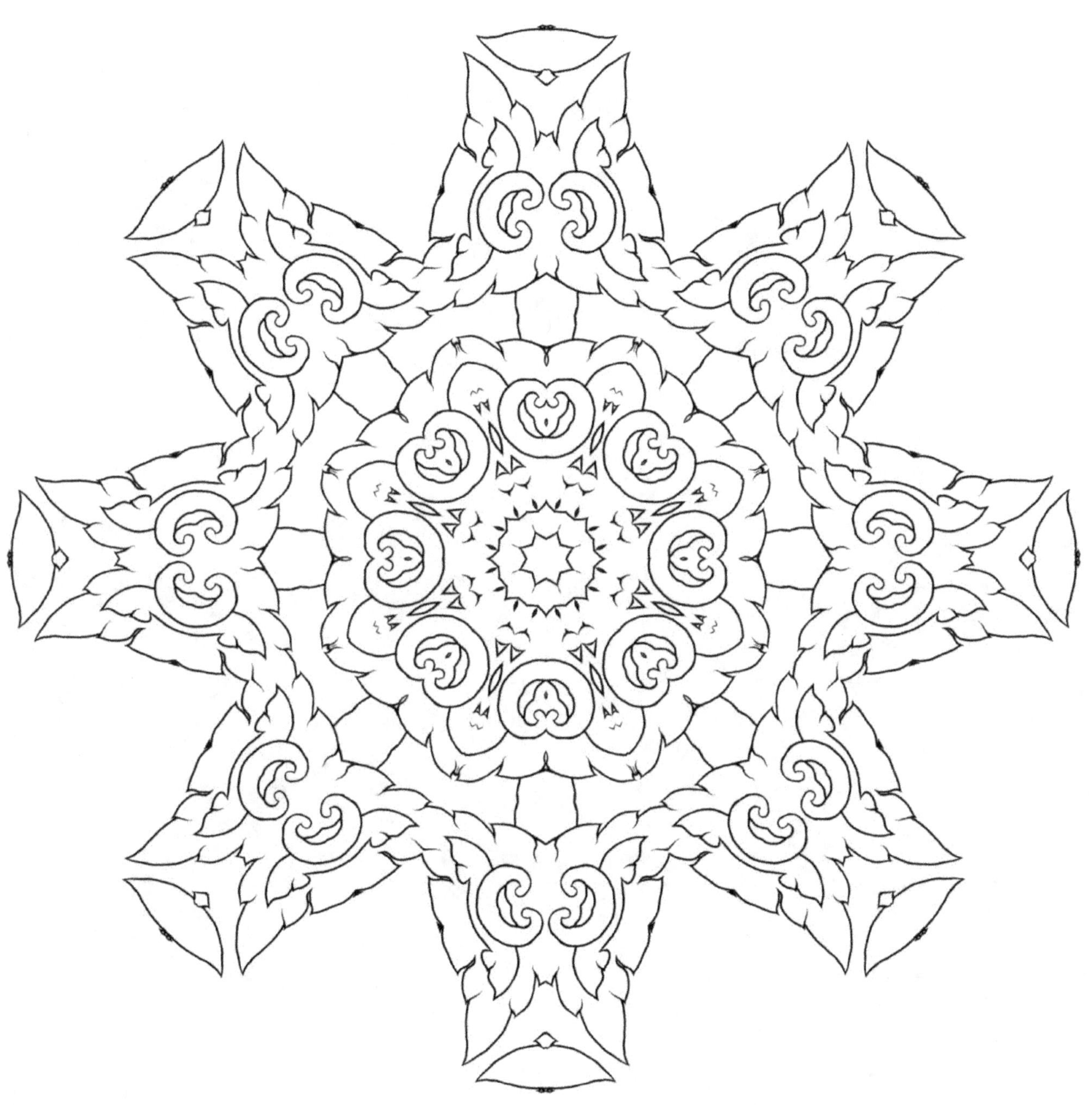

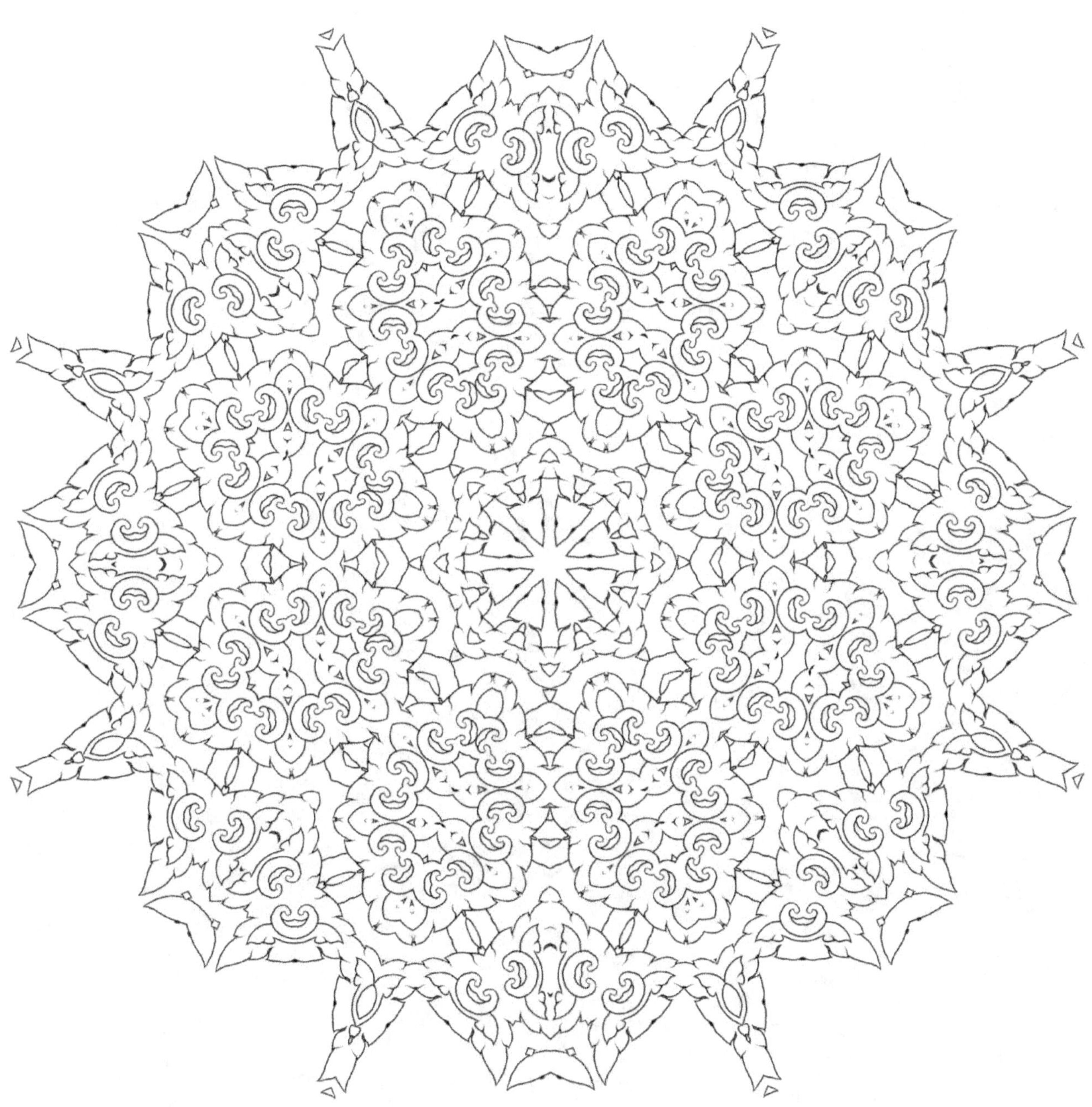

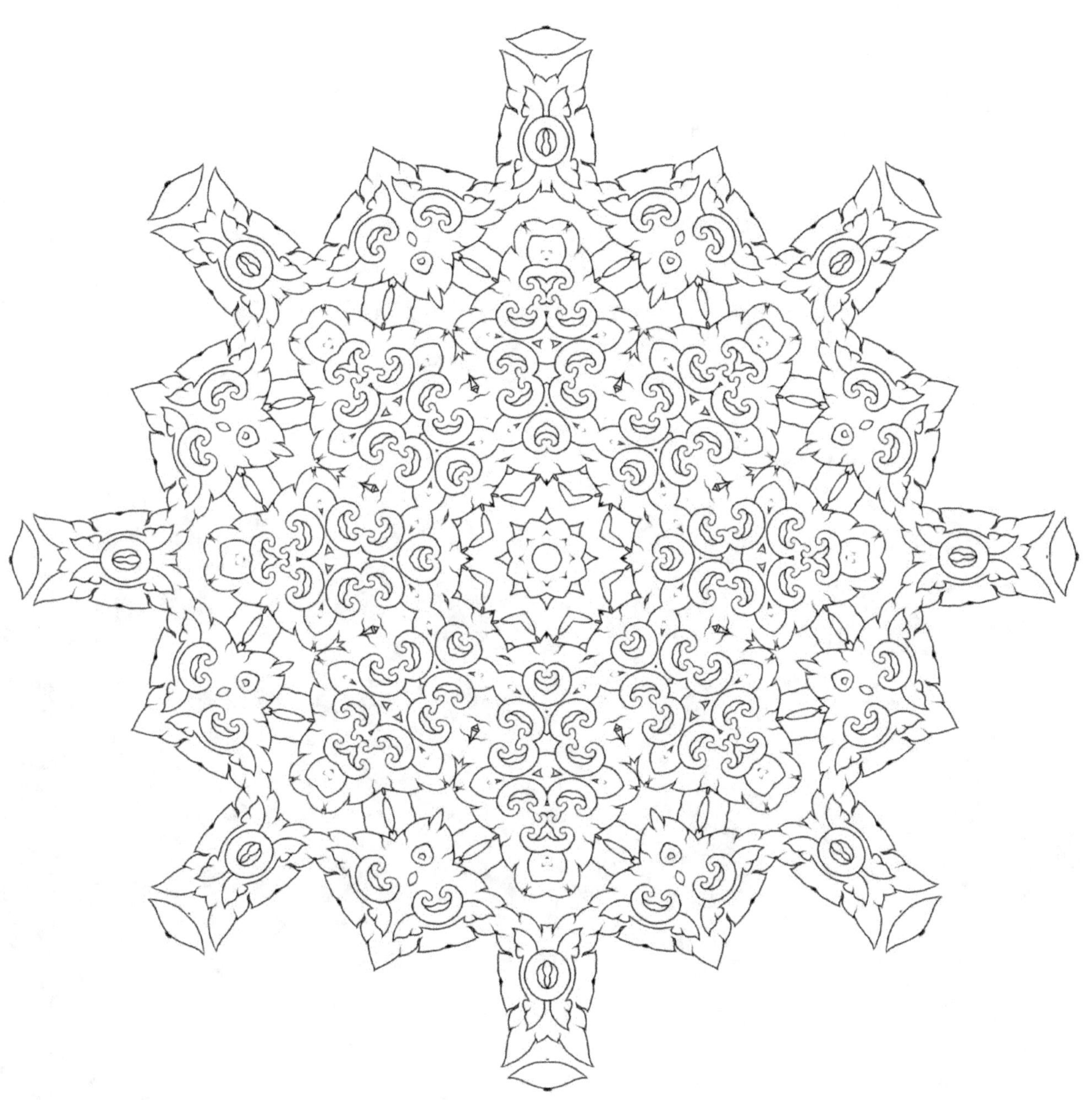

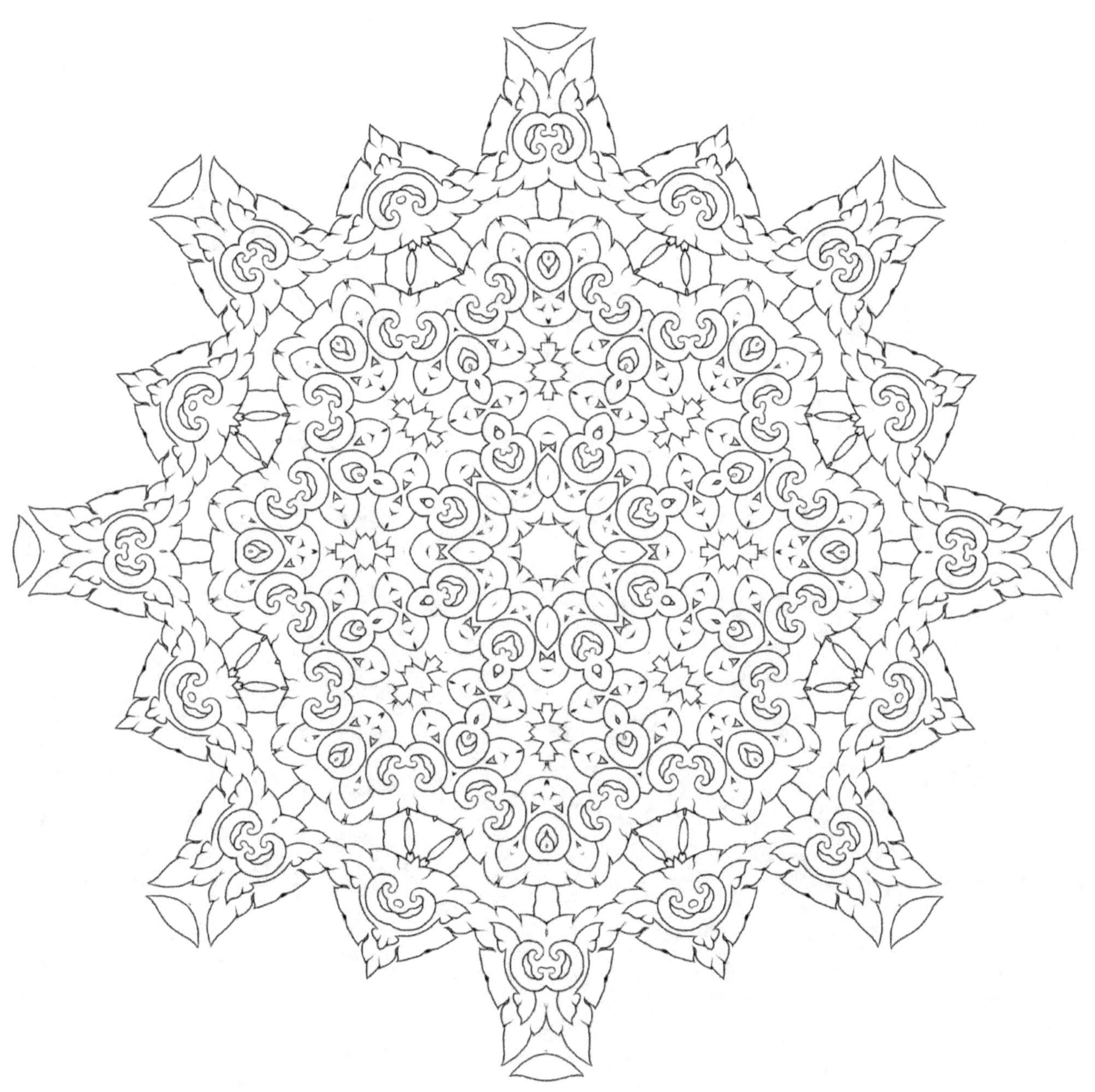

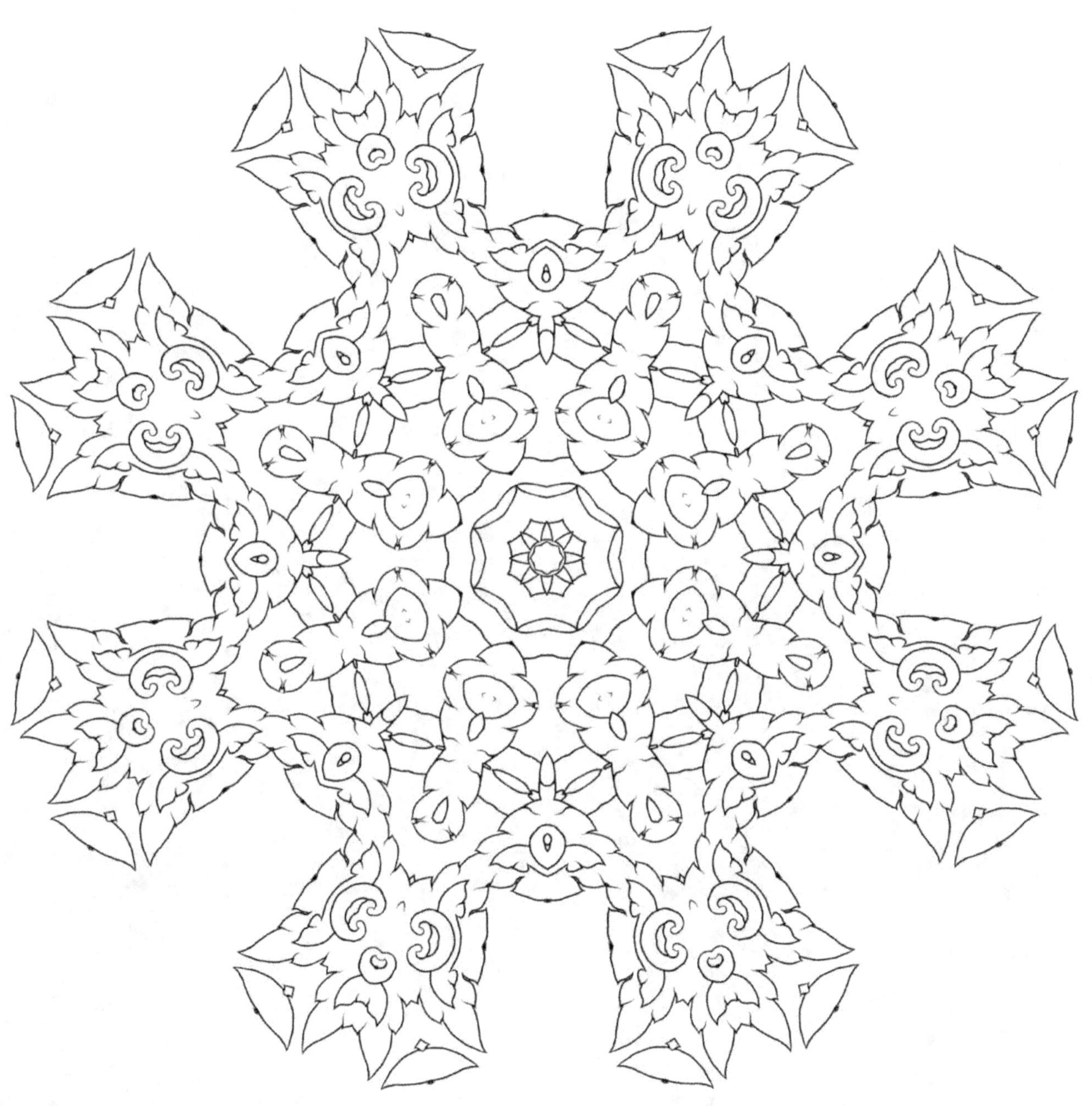

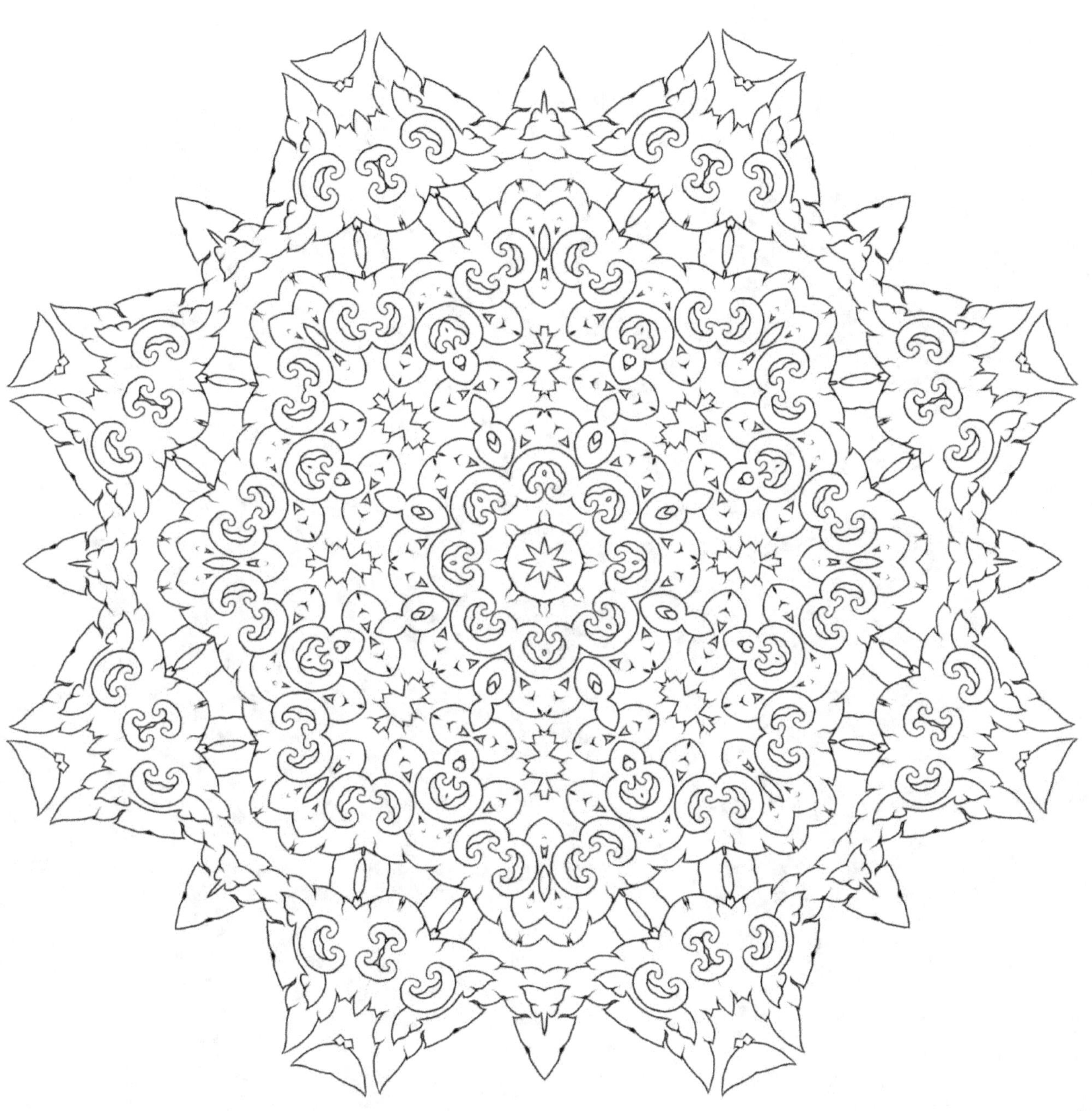

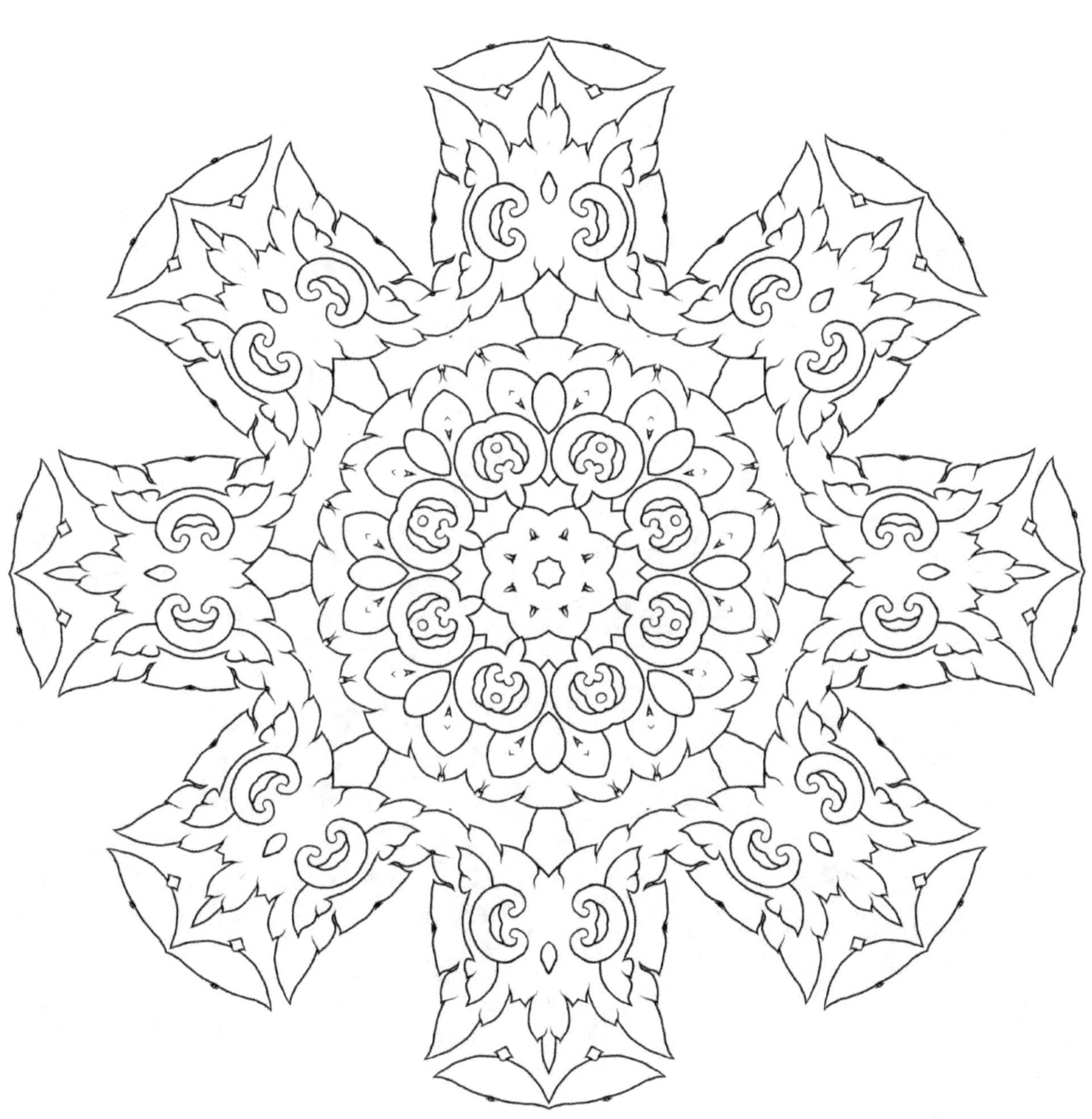

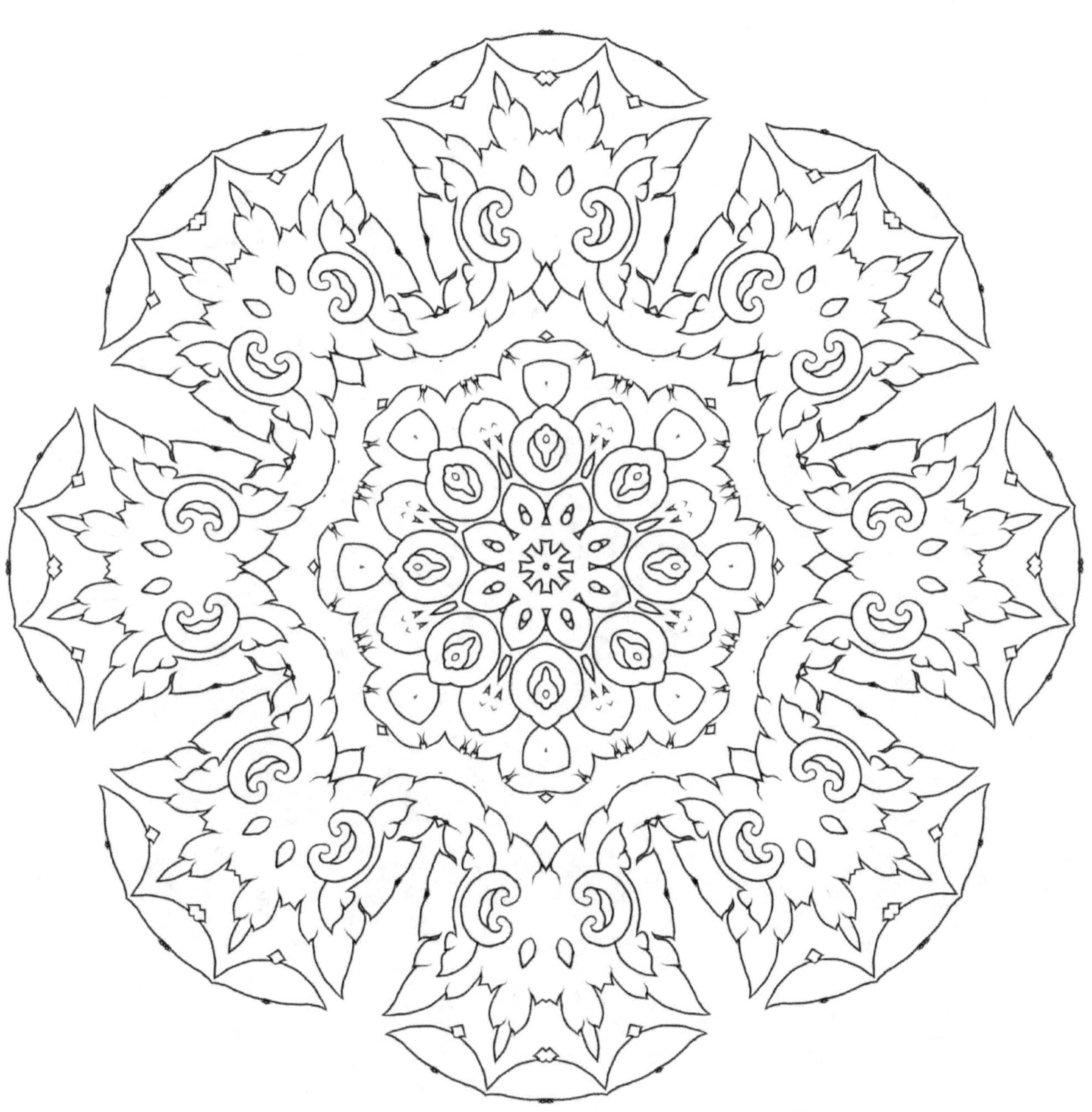

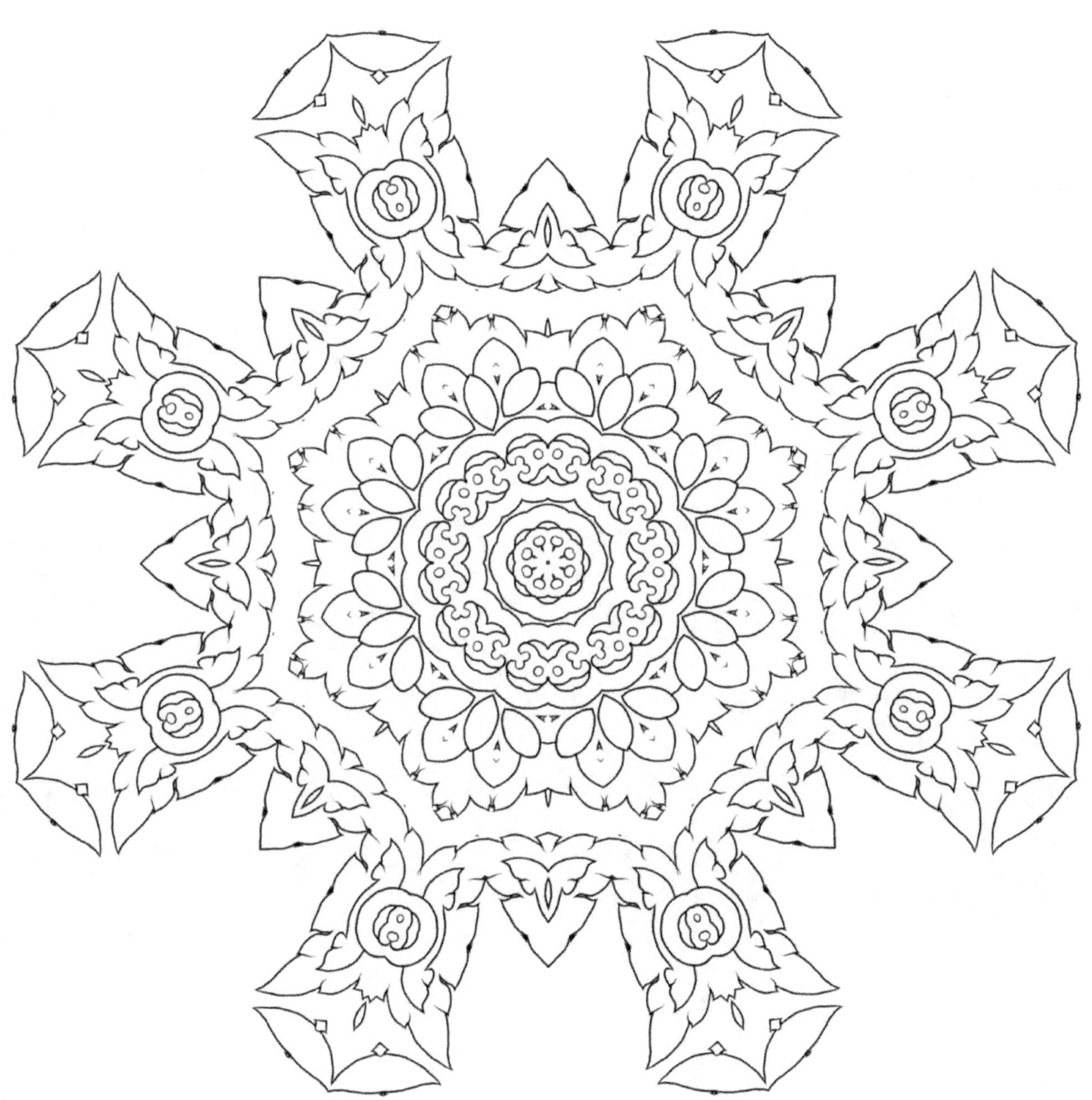

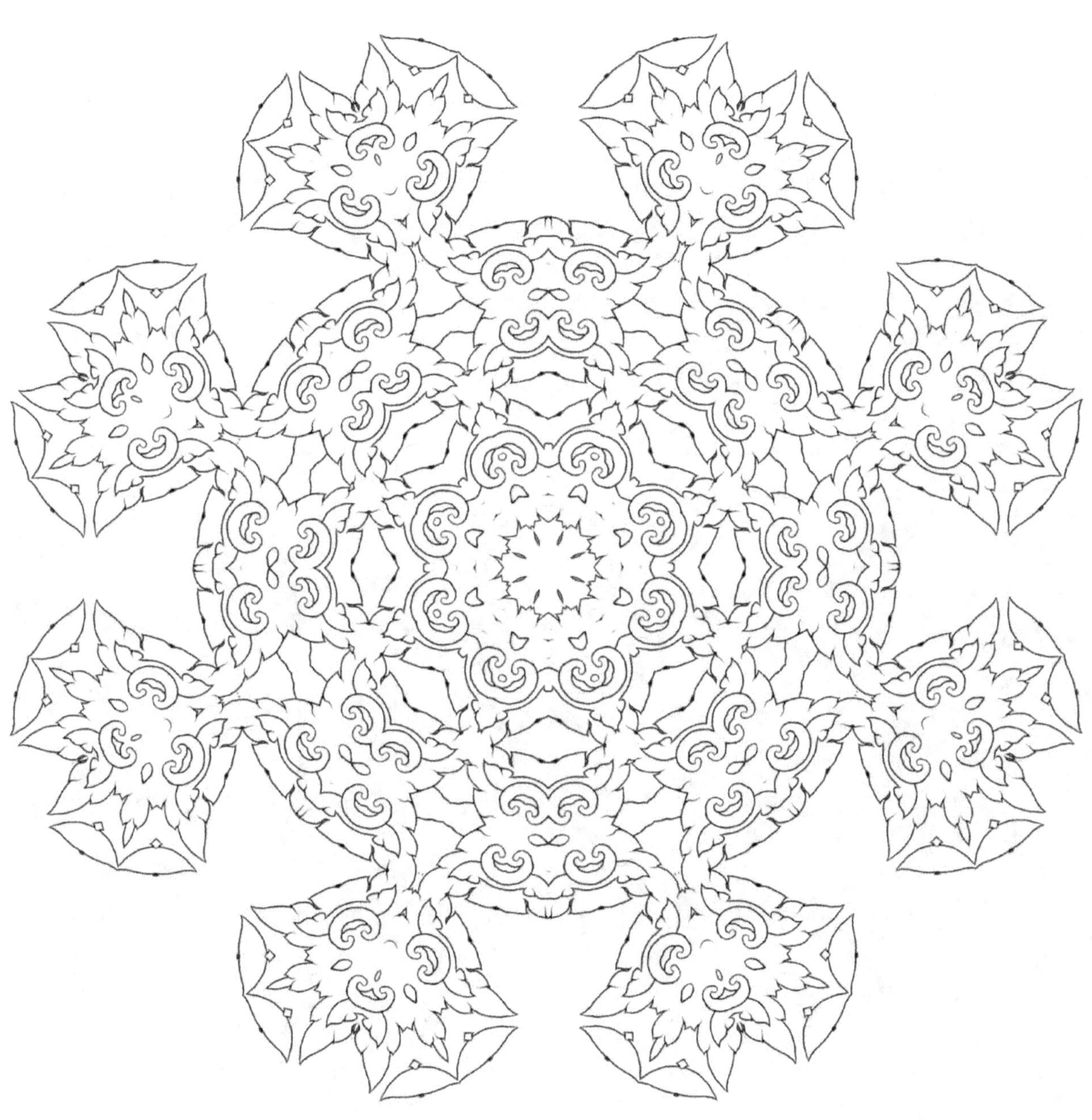

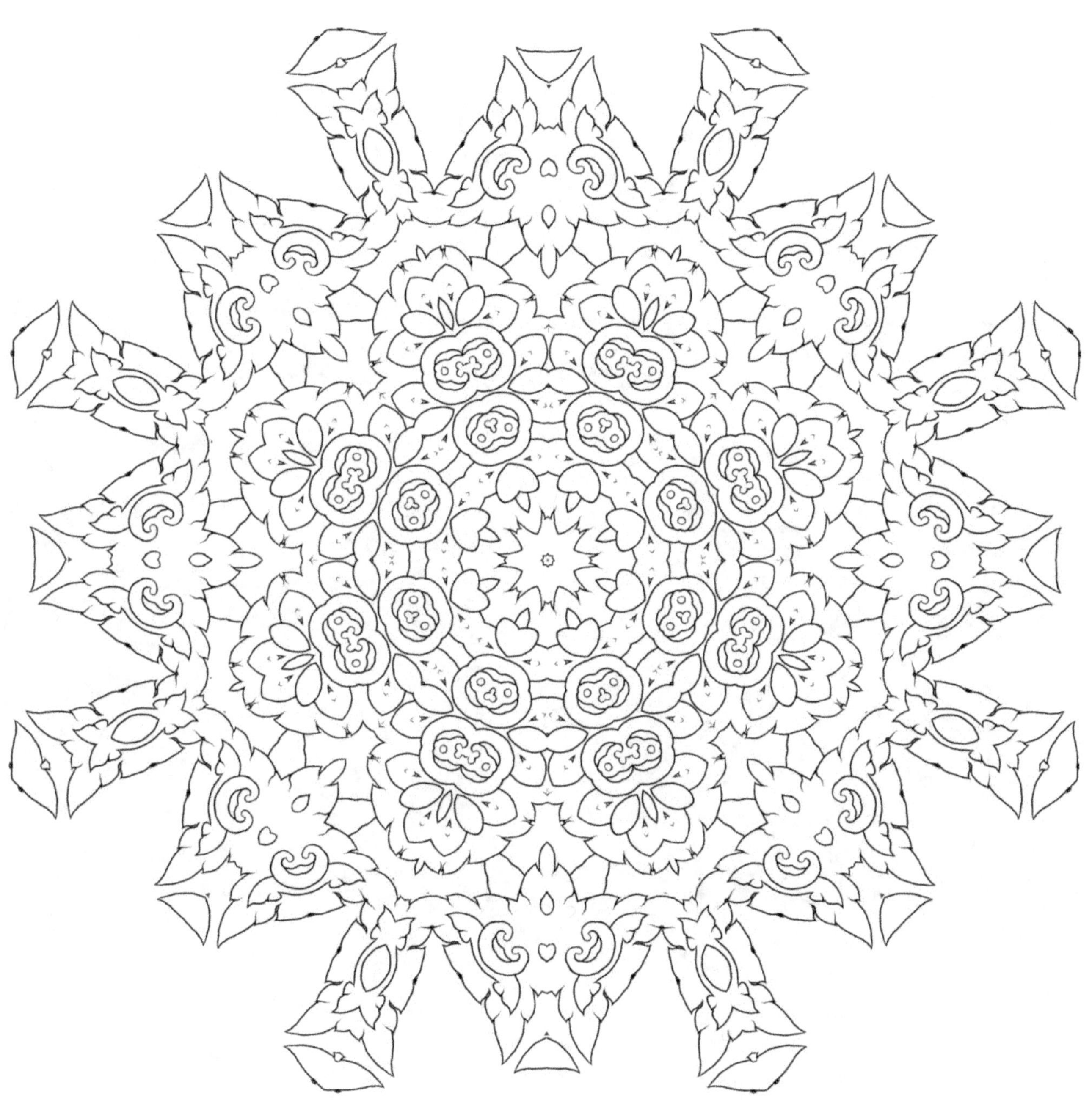

Thank you

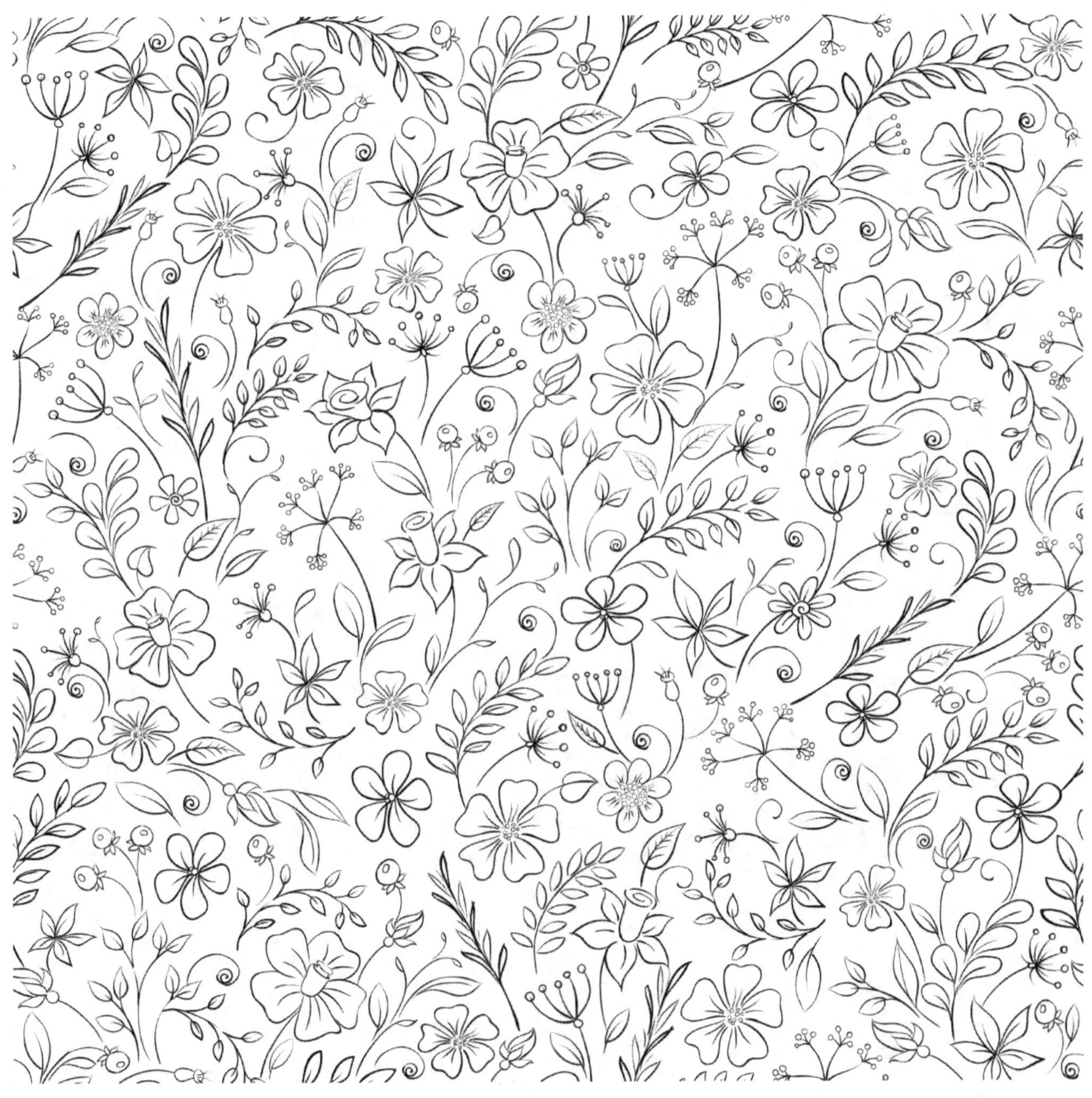